C000184262

GLOSSARY

of

HOUSE PURCHASE AND RENOVATION TERMS

FRENCH-ENGLISH and ENGLISH-FRENCH

compiled by

ALAN S. LINDSEY

HADLEY PAGER INFO

Fourth Edition 2000
Reprinted 2001
Reprinted 2002
Reprinted 2003
Reprinted 2004

ISBN 1-872739-08-3

(ISBN 1-872739-04-0 Third Edition 1996)

HADLEY PAGER INFO
Leatherhead, Surrey, England

FOREWORD

Since publication of the Third Edition of this Glossary in 1996 it has remained a popular vocabulary resource for many buyers and prospective buyers of property in France. Now with the turn of the century, and indeed of the millenium, the opporunity has arrived for an upgrading and a revision of the Glossary to produce a Fourth Edition. The total coverage has been increased to over 2000 words and phrases.

As in previous editions the Glossary provides a guide to French words and phrases used by estate agents and notaires in the description, conveyancing and mortgaging of French properties, including commonly applied legal and financial terms. The range of building terms which are also included makes the glossary useful to owners who wish to proceed with the decoration and renovation of their property.

As is commonly the case in English, many French words often have a variety of meanings. In the present Glossary only those meanings which relate to property are given and therefore the meaning of a word used in a different context should be checked by reference to a good French dictionary. Although a number of legal words and phrases are included in this Glossary a more extensive coverage will be found in my Glossary of French Legal Terms. It should be remembered that French legal terms can have a variety of nuances and where translation of legal documents is concerned experienced advice should be sought from a bilingual solicitor or notaire.

Once again I am greatly indebted to my wife Hazel for her considerable help in the preparation of the text for this revised edition. All errors of omission or translation are mine alone and I welcome any suggestions for improvements in future editions.

A.S.L.

Abbreviations Used

adj	adjective	admin	administration
f	feminine noun	agric	agricultural
m	masculine noun	archit	architectural
pl	plural noun	colloq	colloquial
v	verb	constr	construction
		elect	electrical
		mech	mechanical

FRENCH-ENGLISH

A

abattement *m* deduction; discount; allowance; write-off
- abattement forfaitaire = standard deduction

abonné *m* consumer (gas, electricity); subscriber

abonnement *m* 1 subscription; 2 rate; standing charge (gas/water supply); 3 rental (telephone, flat etc)

abri *m* shelter; cover; shed; protection
- abri à vélos = bicycle shed
- abri pour la voiture = carport

acajou *m* mahogany
- en acajou = made of mahogany

accusé *m* **de réception** acknowledgement of receipt (of letter, etc)

acheter *v* buy (to); purchase (to); acquire (to)
- acheter un appartement clés en main = to buy a flat ready for immediate occupation

acheteur *m*; **acheteuse** *f* purchaser; buyer; vendee

achèvement *m* completion
- en cours d'achèvement; en voie d'achèvement = nearing completion; being completed

achever *v* finish (to); end (to); complete (to)

acier *m* steel
- acier à béton = reinforcing steel (for concrete)
- acier doux = mild steel
- acier fondu = cast steel
- acier inoxydable = stainless steel
- acier moulé = cast (moulded) steel

acompte *m* deposit; instalment; payment on account (note: a deposit designated 'un acompte' on a property purchase usually indicates that neither party can withdraw from the contract (see also dédit))
- laisser/verser un acompte = pay/make a deposit or down payment

acquéreur *m* purchaser; buyer

acquérir *v* acquire (to); purchase (to)

acquisition *f* purchase; acquisition; buying
- prix d'acquisition = purchase price

acte *m* certificate; legal document; deed (see also extrait)
- acte de naissance/mariage = birth/marriage certificate
- acte de l'état civil = birth, marriage or death certificate
- acte définitif = final conveyance document
- acte notarié = notarised deed
- projet d'acte = draft conveyance document

acte *m* **authentique** formal deed (of sale); deed of conveyance; deed executed by a notaire

acte *m* **de vente** final conveyance document; formal deed (of sale); (acte authentique de vente)

acte *m* **sous seing privé** private agreement by a document not legally certified

adresse *f* address
- adresse postale = postal address

affaissement *m* subsidence; sagging; sinking (eg of walls)
- affaissement de terrain = subsidence
- affaissements des sols = subsidence

AFNOR; Association Française de Normalisation French Standards Association

agence *f* agency; branch office
- agence immobilière = estate agency

agent *m* **immobilier** estate agent

agglomération *f* 1 town; built-up area; conurbation; 2 agglomeration

aggloméré *m*; **agglo** *(abb)* 1 agglomerate block (eg breeze block, concrete block); 2 chipboard; particle board; 3 fuel briquette

agrandissement *m* extension

aire *f* area
- aire de loisirs = recreation area
- aire de repos = lay-by; rest area

aisance *f* ease; facility
- l'aisance financière/matérielle = financial security
- see also 'fosse'

alignement *m* alignment

aligner *v* align (to)

alimentation *f* 1 supply; feeding; supplying; 2 food; groceries
- alimentation en eau = water supply
- alimentation en électricité = electricity supply
- alimentation en énergie = power supply
- alimentation en gaz = gas supply

allumage *m* lighting (fire); switching on (electricity); turning on (gas)

allumer *v* light (to) (a fire, cigar etc); switch on (to) (light, radio etc); prime (to) (a pump)
- s'allumer = to switch (itself) on (light,

heating etc)

aluminium *m* aluminium

aménagement *m* fitting-out; converting; conversion; development

aménager *v* convert (to); fit out (to); equip (to) ; lay out (to); plan (to) ; develop (to)
- à aménager = for conversion
- route non aménagée = non-made up road

ameublement *m* furniture; furnishing
- articles d'ameublement = furnishings

amiable *adj* amicable
- vente à l'amiable = private sale; sale by private agreement

amorcer *v* prime (to) (a pump); start/begin (to) (eg building)

ampoule *f* bulb (electric light)
- ampoule à baïonnette = bayonet fitting bulb
- ampoule à vis = screw in bulb

ancien, ancienne *adj*; **ancien** *m* old; former; ancient
- ancien propriétaire = previous owner
- l'ancien = the older property
- logement en ancien = old house; no longer a new house

ancre f de mur wall tie; wall anchor

année f de construction year of construction

annexe *f* **1** annexe; extension (to a building); **2** appendix; annexe; supplement (to a document); **3** schedule (to a contract)

appartement *m* apartment; flat
- plante d'appartement = houseplant
- appartement témoin = show flat
- appartement de standing = luxury apartment

appentis *m* lean-to; sloping roof; penthouse roof; shed

apport *m* contribution; investment; supply; provision
- apport d'eau potable = supply of drinking water
- apport personel = cash deposit; personal financial contribution
- les apports = goods and property

approvisionnement *m* d'eau water supply

apurement *m* audit; balancing; discharge or settlement (of debt)

arbre *m* **1** tree; **2** shaft; axle; spindle (mech)
- arbre chablis = fallen tree
- arbre d'agrément = ornamental tree
- arbre moteur = driving shaft
- arbre sur pied = standing tree

architecte *m* architect
- architecte d'intérieur = interior designer

architecture *f* moderne modern architecture

ardoise *f* **1** slate (roof); **2** unpaid bill
- couverte en ardoises = roofed with slates
- couvrir un toit d'ardoises = to slate a roof

ardoiser *v* slate (to)
- ardoisé,-e *adj* = slate-coloured

are *m* one hundred square metres
(one hectare = 100 ares = 10,000 square metres = 2.471 acres)

aréage *m* measuring area of land in ares

armoire *f* cupboard; wardrobe
- armoire à linge = linen cupboard
- armoire vitrée = glass-fronted cupboard

arpentage *m* land surveying

arpenteur *m* surveyor (land)
- chaine d'arpenteur = (surveyor's) chain; chain measure

arrêté *m* order; administrative order or decree
- arrêté de compte = settlement of account
- arrêté municipal = bye-law

arrhes *fpl* deposit
- verser des arrhes = to put down or pay a deposit

arrière *m* back; rear
- arrière-cour *f* = backyard
- arrière-cuisine *f* = scullery; pantry

arriéré,-e *adj* overdue; in arrears; backward
- en arriéré = owing/overdue
- loyer arriéré = back rent
- paiement arriéré = overdue payment

artisan *m* craftsman; artisan

ascenseur *m* lift; elevator

assainissement *m* draining; cleansing; sanitation; sewage disposal
- assainissement d'habitation = house drainage

assèchement *m* draining; drainage; emptying; drying out

assembler *v* assemble (to); join (to); joint (to)

assujettir *v* secure (to); subject to (to); make fast (to)
- assujetti à l'impot = subject or liable to tax

assurance *f* insurance; assurance
- assurance au tiers = third party insurance
- assurance-incendie = insurance against fire risk
- police d'assurance = insurance policy
- prime d'assurance = insurance premium

assurance *f* **dommage(s)-ouvrage** insurance against building faults (usually covers 10 years following construction of house)

assurance *f* **multirisque(s) habitation** comprehensive household insurance

astreinte *f* constraint; penalty ; daily fine for delay (in completing a contract)

atelier *m* workshop; studio; workroom

attestation *f* certificate

avant-contrat *m* preliminary agreement; preliminary contract (eg promesse unilatérale d'achat)
- avant-contrat synallagmatique = compromis de vente

avant-projet *m* draft project; draft scheme; proposed plan; pilot study; preliminary version

avenant *m* additional clause; endorsement; rider; amendment (to a contract)

avocat *m*; **avocate** *f* advocate; barrister; lawyer
- l'Ordre des Avocats = Association of Lawyers

avoir *m* asset(s); holdings; property; estate

ayant-droit *m*; **ayants-droit** *pl*; **ayant-cause** *m* assign; assignee; legal successor; beneficiary; eligible party
- ayants-droit = rightful claimants/successors

B

bac *m* tub; sink
- bac à laver = washtub; deep sink
- bac à sable = sand pit; sand tray
- bac de douche = shower tray
- évier avec deux bacs = double sink unit

badigeon *m* whitewash; distemper; colour wash
- badigeon blanc = whitewash

badigeonner *v* distemper (to); whitewash (to); colourwash (to)

baie *f* opening; bay
- baie de fenêtre = window opening
- baie vitrée = picture window; bay window
- fenêtre en baie = bay window

baignoire *f* bath; bathtub
- baignoire sabot = hip-bath

bail *m*; **baux** *mpl* lease
- bail à loyer = rental lease; house-letting lease
- bail commercial = commercial lease
- faire un bail = draw up a lease

- locataire à bail = leaseholder
- location à bail = leasehold
- prendre à bail = to lease
- bail emphytéotique = long duration lease (18-99 years)

balai *m* broom

balayer *v* sweep (to)

balcon *m* balcony

ballon *m* **d'eau chaude** hot water tank

barème *m* scale of charges; table; list
- barème de prix = price list
- barème des impôts = tax scale
- barème des tarifs = scale of charges

bastide *f* 1 country house (S. France); fortlet; 2 square stone house
- bastidon *m* = small bastide

bâtiment *m* building; house
- le bâtiment = the building trade
- bâtiments d'élevage = livestock buildings
- bâtiments d'exploitation = farm buildings or sheds
- bâtiment restauré = restored building

bâtir *v* build (to); construct (to); erect (to)
- terrain à bâtir = building land/site
- zone bâtie = built-up area

bâtisse *f* masonry; bricks and mortar; building; house (colloq)

béton *m* concrete
- béton armé = reinforced concrete
- béton précontraint = prestressed concrete
- sol en béton = concrete floor

bétonnière *f* cement/concrete mixer

bien *m* possession; estate; property; (pl) goods
- biens d'équipement ménager = household goods
- biens immeubles/biens immobliers = real estate/property
- biens privés = private property

bilan *m* 1 appraisal; assessment; 2 balance sheet; statement of accounts
- bilan provisoire = provisional estimate
- dresser/établir un bilan = to draw up a balance sheet
- faire le bilan de = to take stock of

bitume *m* bitumen; asphalt; pitch; tar
- papier bituminé = bituminized paper

blindage *m* 1 sheeting (wood or metal); 2 shoring up; 3 screening (elect)

blinder *v* timber (to); shore up (to); screen (to) (elect)

7

bloc *m* block; unit
- bloc-cuisine *m* = kitchen unit
- bloc-evier *m* = sink unit

blocage *m* **1** clamping; locking; **2** rubble work; filling-in (of wall); **3** cement block foundation
- blocageux, blocageuse (adj) = rubbly

bois *m* wood; timber; woodland
- bois blanc = whitewood/deal
- bois contreplaqué = plywood
- bois déjeté/déversé = warped timber
- bois impregné = impregnated wood; treated wood
- bois traité = treated wood
- bois vermoulu = worm-eaten wood
- bois vert = green wood; unseasoned wood

boiserie *f* panelling; wainscoting; woodwork
- boiser *v* = to panel (in wood)

boîte *f* à fusibles fuse box

boîte *f* à ordures dustbin; rubbish bin

boîte *f* de derivation; boîte *f* de jonction junction box (elect); connecting box (elect)
- boîte de derivation à bornes de serrage = junction box with screw connectors

bon état *m* good condition (of a property)
- en bon état = in good repair

bordereau *m* note; list; docket; slip
- bordereau de crédit = cedit note
- bordereau de livraison = delivery note
- bordereau de versement = paying-in slip

bornage *m* boundary marking; demarcation

borne *f* **1** boundary stone or marker; limit; **2** terminal (elect)

bosquet *m* small wood; spinney; grove; copse

bouche *f* d'aération air inlet; air brick
- bouche d'aération à lames = louvred grille

bouche *f* d'égout drain (bottom outlet); street gulley

bouche *f* d'incendie fire hydrant

bouche *f* de ventilation air vent

bouchon *m* stopper; plug; cork; bung
- bouchon à vis = screwed plug/cap

branchement *m* connection; connecting-up; branching; branch-pipe; junction; tapping; plugging-in; installation
- branchement sur le secteur = connection to local electricity supply

bricolage *m* DIY, do-it-yourself (materials); do-it-yourself (job, activity)
- materiaux de bricolage = DIY materials

bricoler *v* do odd jobs (to); do-it-yourself

(DIY) (to); do repairs (to); potter (to)

bricoleur *m* handyman; do-it-yourselfer

bricoleuse *f* handywoman; do-it-yourselfer

brosse *f* brush; paintbrush
- brosse en chiendent = scrubbing brush
- brosse métallique = wire brush

bruit *m* noise; sound
- niveau de bruit = noise level
- pondération des bruits = noise rating
- réduction de bruit = noise reduction

brut,-e *adj* **1** crude; raw; untreated (eg oil); **2** gross (eg weight, cost)

buanderie *f* laundry room; utility room; wash-house

bureau *m* desk; study (room); office
- bureau de poste = post office
- bureau des contributions = tax office
- pendant les heures de bureau = during office hours

bureau *m* de conservation des hypothèques Mortgage Registry; Land Charges Registry
- bureau de conservation des hypothèques = Land Registry
- bureau des hypothèques = Land Registry
- conservateur/conservatrice des hypothèques = Land Registrar; Mortgage Registrar
- conservation des hypothèques = Mortgage Office of Land Registry

C

cabanon *m* cabin; small hut; chalet; maisonnette (Provence)

cabinet *m* office; study; closet; cabinet (furniture)
- cabinet d'étude = study
- cabinet de débarras = boxroom/lumber room
- cabinet de toilette = bathroom; cloakroom; dressing room
- les cabinets = toilet/loo

câblage *m* de circuit circuit wiring

câble *m* cable; heavy-duty flex
- câble de mise à la terre = earthing cable/wire
- câble électrique = electric cable
- câble enterré = buried cable
- câble métallique = wire rope; stranded wire
- câble multifilaire = multi-wire cable

cadastre *m* land registry; cadastral register; cadastral survey

campagne *f* countryside; open country
- chemin de campagne = country lane
- maison de campagne = house/cottage in the countryside

canalisation *f* pipes; main pipe; pipework; ground level pipework; canalisation; cables (elect); conduit (wiring/cable)

caniveau *m* 1 gutter (road); drainage channel; 2 cable duct

capacité *f* capacity; legal capacity; legal status
- capacité en droit = basic legal qualification

capital *m* capital; funds

carneau *m* flue
- carneau de chaudière = boiler flue

carreau *m* tile; tiled floor; pane (window glass)
- carreau au/de mur = wall tile
- carreau de faïence = ceramic wall tile
- carreau de liège = cork tile
- carreau de pierre = flagstone
- carreau de plâtre = plaster block (for partitions)
- carreau de sol = floor tile
- carreau de vitre = window pane

carrelage *m* tiles; tiling; tile floor
- carrelage (de) sol = floor tiles/tiling
- carrelage mural de cuisine = kitchen wall tiles/tiling

carreler *v* tile (to)

carreleur *m* tiler

carte *f* **de séjour** resident's permit

caution *f* guarantee; security; bail bond; deposit of guarantee
- verser une caution de mille euros = to lay down a security/guarantee of a thousand euros

cave *m* cellar; storeroom (usually at ground floor level); vault; basement (of house)
- cave voûtée = vault; vaulted cellar
- caveau *m* = (small) cellar

cellier *m* storeroom

centre ville *m* town centre

certificat *m* **d'urbanisme** certificate issued by local authority stating planning and building status for specified property

certificat *m* **de changement de résidence** certificate of change of residence

certificat *m* **de conformité** certificate of conformity (issued by the local authority to confirm building work is in accordance with the terms of the 'permis de construire')

cession-bail *f* leaseback

chai *m* wine cellar; wine and spirit store; vat room; shed

chambre *f* bedroom
- chambre à coucher = bedroom; bedroom suite
- chambre d'amis = spare/guest room
- chambre de bonne = maid's room

champ *m* field
- champ de courses = racecourse
- la vie aux champs = life in the country

chantier *m* building site; roadworks
- chantier de construction = building site
- ouverture du chantier = start of building work

chape *f* **ciment** cement covering; screed

charges *fpl* **d'un appartement** service charges (payable by tenants of flats etc)
- charges locatives = maintenance or service charges

charnière *f* hinge; butt-hinge

charpente *f* frame(work) (of house, building); skeleton
- bois de charpente = timber
- charpente en bois = carpentry

charpentier *m* carpenter (assembly of roof timbers, etc); (see also menuisier)

chartreuse *f* lone cottage or lodge; house in isolated area; manor house

chasse *f* **d'eau** flushing cistern of WC
- tirer la chasse = flush the toilet

châssis *m* frame (of window)
- châssis de charpente = outer frame; open framework (timber)

château *m* castle; country mansion; a house associated with a vineyard

châtière *f* roof vent; cat entry (in door)

chaudière *f* boiler
- chaudière à eau chaude = hot water boiler
- chaudière à gaz = gas boiler
- chaudière cylindrique = cylindrical boiler

chauffage *m* heating
- chauffage à air chaud = hot air heating
- chauffage à air pulsé = warm air heating
- chauffage électrique/à l'electricité = electric heating
- chauffage à pompe à chaleur = heating by heat pump
- chauffage au charbon = coal-fired heating; solid fuel heating

- chauffage au fuel = fuel-oil heating
- chauffage au gaz ville = gas heating
- chauffage au mazout = oil-fired heating
- chauffage central = central heating
- chauffage solaire = solar heating
- chauffage électrique par accumulation = electric storage heating
- chauffage par le sol/sous-sol = under-floor heating

chauffagiste *m* heating engineer

chauffe-eau *m* water-heater
- chauffe-bain = water-heater; geyser
- chauffe-eau à élément chauffant = immersion heater
- chauffe-eau à gaz = gas water heater
- chauffe-eau électrique = electric water heater
- chauffe-plats = dish-warmer

chaumière *f* cottage; thatched cottage

chaussée *f* road; roadway
- chaussée pavée = cobbled road

chemin *m* path; lane; track
- chemin d'accès = access path
- chemin de fer = railway
- chemin de traverse = path across a field

cheminée *f* 1 chimney (stack); 2 fireplace; mantelpiece
- la souche de cheminée = chimney stack (above roof level)

chêne *m* oak

chéneau *m* gutter (roof)

chèque *m* cheque
- chèque barré = crossed cheque
- chèque libellé à l'ordre de l'établissement bancaire = cheque drawn to the order of a bank

chevron *m* rafter

chevronnage *m* rafters (roof); raftering

chrome *m* chromium
- acier chromé = chrome steel
- chromage *m* = chromium plating (process)
- chromé = chromium plated

chute *f* drop; slope; pitch; fall; downfall
- chute de comble = pitch of roof
- chute d'eau = head of water;
- chute de tension = voltage drop

ciment *m* cement
- ciment à prise rapide = quick-setting cement
- ciment armé = reinforced cement
- ciment colle = tile fixing adhesive cement

circuit *m* circuit (elect)
- circuit électrique = electric circuit

- mettre en circuit = to connect up

citerne *f* tank; water tank; rain-water tank; cistern

claire-voie *f*; **claires-voies** *fpl* 1 opening; open-work ; open-work fence; lattice; 2 skylight
- couverture à claire-voie = method used to protect walls from rain

clause *f* clause; article; provision; stipulation
- clause aléatoire = aleatory/chance- dependent clause
- clause compromissoire = arbitration clause
- clause de style = standard or set clause
- clause dérogatoire = escape clause; overriding clause
- clause facultative = optional clause
- clause particulière = special condition clause
- clause pénale = penalty clause
- clause résolutoire = resolutive clause; determination clause (for a contract); cancellation clause
- clause suspensive = suspensive or let-out clause; conditional clause

clé ou clef *f* key; spanner; wrench
- clef à douille = box-spanner

climatisation *f* air conditioning

cloison *f* partition; partition wall; division
- cloison en bois = wood partition
- cloison extensible = folding door/divider
- cloison mitoyenne = partition wall
- cloisonnage *m* = partitioning
- contre-cloison = partition liner; partition placed against a wall

clos *m* field (enclosed); vineyard
- clos de pommiers = apple orchard

clos,-e *adj* enclosed; closed; shut; finished

clôture *f* fence; fencing; paling; hedge; wall; enclosure
- clôture de bornage = boundary fence
- grille de clôture = surrounding railing
- mur de clôture = outer/surrounding wall

clou *m* nail (see also pointe)
- clou à deux pointes = staple; wire-staple

clouer *v* nail (to)

coffret *m* **de distribution; coffret de répartition** distribution box

coin *m* corner
- coin-cuisine *m* = corner kitchen; kitchenette
- coin-repas *m* = dinette

collecteur *m* receiver (tank); collector
- collecteur d'impôts = tax collector

- collecteur principal = main sewer
- égout collecteur = main drain (sewage); main sewer
- grand collecteur = main sewer

colombage *m* half-timbered
- maison à colombage = half-timbered house

colombier *m* dovecot; pigeon house

coloris *m* colour; shade
- carte de coloris *f* = shade card

comble *m*; **combles** *mpl* roof; roof space; roof (cover and frame); roof timbers; roof trussing
- comble d'un bâtiment= roof (of a building)
- comble mansardé = mansard roof; curb roof; French roof
- les combles = the attic; the loft; roof space

communauté *f* community
- communauté de biens = joint estate
- communauté urbaine = urban district; urban community
- en communauté = joint ownership (of property)
- la Communauté européenne = The European Community

commune *f* commune; town; village; district; parish
- commune rurale/urbaine = rural/urban district

compromis *m* **de vente** bilateral agreement to sell/buy; preliminary contract to sell or buy

comptabilité *f* book-keeping; accounting; accountancy; accounts department

comptable *m/f* accountant; book-keeper

compte *m* account; count; calculation
- compte en banque = bank account
- compte spécifié = itemised account
- relevé de compte = statement of account

compte-rendu *m* report; progress report (eg of building work); minutes (of meeting)
- compte rendu d'essai = test report
- le compte rendu d'une réunion = the minutes of a meeting

compteur *m* meter; counter
- compteur à gaz = gas meter
- compteur d'eau = water meter
- compteur d'électricité = electricity meter
- compteur électrique = electricity supply meter

condensation *f* condensation
- condensation par surface = surface condensation

condition *f* condition; stipulation; term of

contract
- condition particuliére = specific/special condition
- condition résolutoire = resolutory/determinative condition
- condition suspensive = suspensive/conditional/let-out term
- conditions d'un contrat = terms of a contract
- conditions générales = general conditions/terms

conduit *m* pipe; conduit; cable duct
- conduit de cheminée = flue
- conduit de fumée = flue; smoke-pipe
- conduit en grés = earthenware drainpipe

conduite *f* duct; ducting; conduit; pipe; conduct

confection *f* making; preparation; preparing; drawing up (of deed, will); compilation (of inventory)

conseiller *m* **juridique**; **conseillère** *f* **juridique** legal adviser; lawyer

consignation *f* deposit (of money); consignment (of merchandise)

consommation *f* **de courant** current consumption (elect)

constat *m* certified report; report or statement (spoken or written)
- constat à l'amiable = jointly agreed statement for insurance purposes
- constat d'accident = accident report
- constat parasitaire = professional report on whether property is free or not of parasites (termites, capricorn beetle, etc)

constructeur *m* builder; constructor
- constructeur de maisons = house-builder

constructible *adj* physical conditions and official authorisation permits construction
- le terrain est constructible = construction is possible on the site

construction *f* building; construction; structure
- en construction = under construction

construire *v* build (to); construct (to)

contenance *f* content; capacity (eg volume of reservoir); size (of land area)

contrat *m* contract; deed; agreement
- passer un contrat = to enter into/sign an agreement

contrat *m* **de construction** construction contract

contrat *m* **d'entreprise** business contract (eg building work contract); company contract

contrat *m* **de location** rent agreement; tenancy agreement

contrat *m* **de reservation** reservation contract (eg for purchase of a property being built)

contrat *m* **de vente d'immeuble à construire** contract of sale of a building under construction

contrat *m* **synallagmatique** bilateral contract; contract in which both parties are equally bound

contremaître *m*; **contremaîtresse** *f* foreman/ forewoman

contremarche *f* riser (of staircase)

contrevent *m* shutter; brace or strut (carpentry); wind-brace

convertir *v* convert (to); transform (to)
- convertir en = to convert into

copropriété *f* co-ownership; joint ownership
- immeuble en copropriété = block of flats; a condominium
- logement en copropriété = apartment block
- règlements de copropriété = rules of condominium

corps *m* **de bâtiment** main body (of a building); main building; cluster of buildings
- corps de bâtiments = block of buildings
- corps de ferme = farm building(s)
- corps de logis = housing unit; main building

cotisation *f* contribution; subscription; fee; dues

couche *f* layer; coat (of paint, etc)
- couche d'air = air gap (cavity wall)
- couche d'étanchéité = damp-proof course
- couche isolante = insulating layer
- première couche = priming coat
- sous-couche = undercoat (paint)

couleur *f* colour

coupe *f* section; cross-section

coupe-circuit *m* circuit-breaker; fuse; cut-out (elect)
- coupe-circuit à fusible = fuse(d) circuit-breaker

couper *v* cut (to); cut-off (to); switch off (to) (elect)

coupure *f* cut; cutting; power cut
- coupure de courant/d'électricité = power cut

cour *f* yard; courtyard; court
- cour de ferme = farmyard
- cour empierrée = stone courtyard
- cour intérieure = inner courtyard

courant *m* current; power (elect)
- courant alternatif = alternating current

courette *f* small courtyard

coût *m* cost
- coût de conversion = conversion cost
- coût de l'installation = installation cost

couverture *f* roofing; roof; cover
- couverture de chaume = thatched roofing
- couverture en tuiles = tiled roofing

couvreur *m* roof tiler; roofer; slater
- couvreur en ardoise = slater
- couvreur en chaume = thatcher

créancier *m*; **créancière** *f* creditor

crédit *m* credit
- crédit-bail *m* = leasing
- crédit-relais *m* = stand-by credit; short-term bridging loan

crépi *m* rendering; cement rendering; roughcast; masonry paint (textured)
- crépi intérieur = interior wallpaint
- crépi extérieur = exterior wallpaint

crépir *v* render with cement (to); roughcast (to); apply textured masonry paint (to)

crépissage *m* rendering; roughcasting

cuisine *f* kitchen
- cuisine équipée = fitted kitchen

cuisinière *f* cooker; stove; kitchen range
- cuisinière à charbon = solid-fuel stove; coal-fired cooker
- cuisinière à gaz = gas cooker or stove
- cuisinière électrique = electric cooker

cuivre *m* copper

cumulus *m* **électrique** hot water tank with immersion heater

curatelle *f* guardianship; trusteeship

curateur *m*; **curatrice** *f* trustee; guardian; administrator

cuve *f* cistern (water); tank (fuel oil); vat

cuvelage *m*; **cuvellement** *m* lining (eg of a well, cellar); waterproof floor and walls of a basement

cuvette *f* wash-basin, bowl
- cuvette de WC = lavatory pan
- cuvette rotule = ball-socket

D

dallage *m* paving; flagging; pavement

dalle *f* flag; flagstone; paving stone; slab

daller *v* pave (to)

débarras *m* box room; lumber room;

clearance; riddance
- débarras de grenier = attic clearance
- se débarrasser de = to get rid of

décennale *f* ten year guarantee on new property

décharge *f* 1 discharge; outlet; 2 release of debt; receipt; 3 refuse tip; rubbish dump
- décharge des eaux usées = discharge/disposal of waste water

déchetterie *f* waste/scrap disposal depot

déclaration *f* **d'achèvement des travaux** notification that permitted building work has been completed (see also 'le certificat de conformité')

décombres *mpl* (building) rubble or debris

décompte *m* deduction; discount; count; detailed account; statement

décorateur *m*; **décoratrice** *f* decorator
- décorateur d'intérieur = interior decorator

décoration *f* decoration; decorating

dédit *m* forfeit deposit (eg on property purchase) (see also acompte); penalty
- clause de dédit = forfeit clause

déduction *f* 1 deduction; 2 allowance
- déduction faite de .... = after deducting

défaut *m* 1 defect; fault; flaw; 2 default
- défaut caché = latent/hidden defect
- défaut d'entretien = lack of upkeep
- défaut de paiement = default; failure to pay

définitif,définitive *adj* final; definitive; permanent
- acte définitif = final conveyance document
- en définitive = eventually; in fact

défrichage ou défrichement *m* clearing; surface-clearing (of ground, wood etc)

dégagement *m* 1 passage (in apartment); 2 back-door; exit; 3 redemption (eg of mortgage)
- dégagement d'entrée = private entrance
- escalier de dégagement = private staircase
- voie de dégagement = a slip road

dégât *m* damage
- dégâts des eaux = water damage
- évaluer les dégâts = to assess the damage

dégrèvement *m* 1 relief; exemption (from tax); 2 disencumbrance (of a mortgage); 3 abatement
- dégrèvement fiscal = tax relief/tax allowance

délabré *adj* dilapidated (house); crumbling (wall)

délai *m* time-limit; delay; deadline
- délai de livraison = delivery date; terms of delivery

- délai de réflexion = time for consideration; cooling-off time

délestage *m* load-shedding (eg of electricity); power cut

démarche *f* step; procedure
- les démarches nécessaires = the necessary steps

démarrer *v* 1 switch on (to) (electrical appliance); 2 start (to); start up (to)

déménagement *m* removal; moving
- frais de déménagement = removal expenses

demeure *f* residence; dwelling; imposing house with land

démolir *v* demolish (to); pull down (to)

département *m* department (French administrative region)

dépendance *f* outbuilding; dependence
- maison et dépendances = house and outbuildings

dépense *f* 1 expense; expenditure; spending; outlay; 2 consumption (of electricity)
- les dépenses de la maison/du ménage = household expenses

déplacer *v* move (to); shift (to); displace (to)
- se déplacer = to be moved

déposer *v* 1 lodge (to) (a document); 2 lay down (to); 3 dump (to) (rubbish); 4 deposit (to) (money)

dépôt *m* 1 deposit; 2 depository; 3 depot; yard; warehouse
- dépôt de garantie = deposit (as guarantee)
- dépôt d'ordures = (rubbish) dump or tip
- dépôt préalable = advance deposit
- verser un dépôt = to pay a deposit

dépotoir *m* 1 rubbish dump; rubbish tip; 2 sewage works

déroulement *m* progress; development
- déroulement des travaux = progress of building work
- déroulement du contrat = progress of the contract

désordre *m* disorder; irregularity
- les désordres = non-conformities or faults noted after contract work

dessin *m* drawing; design; sketch
- dessin d'architecture = architectural drawing
- dessin de coupe = sectional drawing

dessinateur *m*; **dessinatrice** *f* draughtsman; draughtswoman; designer

dessous de table under the table; sum paid

secretly to the vendor, in addition to the
declared price, in a property deal

destination *f* **d'une batiment** intended use of
a building; purpose for which building is to be
used

destination *f* **du local** usage premises/
dwelling will be put to (eg private or
commercial)

détail *m* detail
- le détail de la facture = a breakdown of the
invoice

détritus *mpl* rubbish; refuse
- détritus de jardin = garden rubbish

deux-pièces *m* two-roomed flat or apartment

devis *m* estimate; quotation; specification
- devis descriptif = detailed estimate;
specification
- devis estimatif = preliminary estimate
- devis préliminaire = outline specification

discuter *v* discuss (to); examine (to) (see also
examiner); haggle (to) (over a price)

disjoncteur *m* trip switch; circuit breaker;
contact breaker (elect)

disposition *f* 1 disposal; 2 draft; 3 provision;
clause; stipulation (legal); 4 lay-out
- disposition de biens = disposal of property
- disposition testamentaire = clause of a will
- dispositions à vue = drawings on an account

document *m* document

domaine *m* estate; property; domain; region
- le Domaine = state-owned property
- Les Domaines = government department
managing state-owned land and property

domicile *m* **principal** principal residence;
main home; registered address
- domicile légal = permanent residence; official
domicile

dommage *m* damage; loss; harm; injury
- dommages et intérêts/dommages-intérêts =
damages (see also assurance dommage-ouvrage)

dommages-ouvrage *m* insurance for building
works (taken out by client)

dossier *m* 1 dossier; documentation; 2 file
- dossier de permis de construire = application
documents and plans required for the 'permis de
construire'

doublage *m* 1 lining; 2 doubling; laying double; 3
plating

double vitrage *m* double glazing

douche *f* 1 shower; 2 drenching; soaking

- bloc-douche *m* = shower unit
- cabine de douche = shower cabinet
- salle de douches = shower-room; showers

douille *f* bulb socket; lamp holder

droit *m* law; right; authority; claim; title; due
- à qui de droit = to whom it may concern
- de droit = of course; by right
- droit de gage = lien
- droit de passage = right of way
- droit de puisage = right to draw water; right
to pump water (from the ground)
- droit écrit = written law; statute law
- droit privé/public = private/public law or
right
- droits d'enregistrement = registration fees;
property transfer registration costs
- droits de préemption = right of precedence of
one purchaser over another at the same
purchase price
- droits de succession = inheritance tax; estate
duties; death duties; probate duty

duplex *m* split-level apartment; maisonette

E

eau *f* water
- eau buvable/potable = drinking water
- eau de distribution = tap water
- eau de ville = town/mains water
- eau douce = fresh water
- eau douce/dure = soft/hard water
- eau froide/chaude = cold/hot water
- eaux ménagères = household waste water
- eaux pluviales; EP = rain water; run-off water
- eaux résiduaires = sewage
- eaux usées; EU = domestic waste water;
sullage
- eaux vannes; EV = foul water; sewage

ébauche *f* rough sketch; sketching out
- ébaucher = to sketch out
- le plan s'ébauche = the plan takes shape

ébéniste *m* cabinet-maker

échafaudage *m* scaffolding

échéance *f* deadline; date of maturity; due date;
expiry; settlement date
- l'échéance d'une police = expiration of a
policy
- payable à l'échéance = payable when due

- venir à échéance = to fall due

échéant *adj* falling due; payable
- le cas échéant = if the case arises; if need be

échelle *f* 1 ladder; 2 scale (eg of map)
- échelle double = (high) stepladder

éclairage *m* 1 lighting (elect); 2 illumination

école *f* school
- école maternelle = nursery school
- école privée = private school (fee-paying)
- école publique = state school

écoulement *m* drainage; flow; outflow
- écoulement d'électricité = flow of electricity
- écoulement naturel = natural drainage
- tuyau/fossé d'écoulement = drainage pipe/ditch

écurie *f* stable

édifice *m* building; edifice
- édifice public = public building

édifier *v* build (to); construct (to); erect (to)

égout *m* sewer; drain
- égout collecteur = main sewer
- égout pluvial = storm drain/sewer
- le tout-à-l'égout = mains drainage
- rèseau d'égouts = sewerage system
- système d'égouts = sewerage system

égout *m* du bord du toit eaves
- égout = eaves
- égout (pente d'un toit) = slope of a roof
- toit à deux égouts = ridge roof

électricien *m* electrician

électricité *f* electricity; electric wiring (colloq.)
- E.D.F. = Électricité de France = French Electricity Board

électroménager *m*; also *adj* household electrical appliances

élément *m* unit; element; component
- éléments compris dans le contrat = items covered by contract
- élément de cuisine = kitchen unit
- éléments de rangement = storage units

élire *v* elect (to)
- élire domicile à = to take up residence in/at

empierrer *v* metal (to); gravel (to) (eg roadway)
- cour empierrée = stone courtyard
- empierrement m = stone layer; hardcore

emprise *f* au sol area of ground (appropriated, acquired or occupied)

emprunt *m* loan; borrowing
- contracter un emprunt = to raise a loan
- emprunt-logement = house purchase loan; mortgage
- route d'emprunt = alternative road; by-pass

emprunter *v* 1 borrow (to); 2 make use of (to); use (to)
- emprunteur *m*; emprunteuse *f* = borrower

en arriéré overdue; owing

en plus in addition
- en plus de cela = in addition to that
- les frais en plus = extra charges

encastrer *v* embed (to); fit flush (to)

enchère *f* bid
- faire une enchère = to make a bid
- vendre aux enchères = to sell by auction

enduit *m* coating; plaster rendering
- enduit de goudron = coating of tar
- enduit de lissage = smooth rendering; smooth coating (of filler; plaster); smoothing plaster or filler
- enduit de rebouchage = filler; stopper; filler rendering

engagement *m* agreement; commitment
- signer un engagement = to sign an agreement

enlèvement *m* removal; collection
- enlèvement des ordures ménagères = collection of household rubbish

énoncé *m* statement; wording; terms; exposition

énoncer *v* express (to); state (to)

ensemble *m* group; set; housing development
- ensemble industriel = industrial estate
- grand ensemble = high-density housing complex or development
- les grands ensembles = high-rise flats; tower blocks
- plan d'ensemble m = housing development plan; site plan; location plan

ensemblier *m* designer (interior)

entrée *f* entrance; entry; hallway

entrepreneur *m* contractor
- entrepreneur de constructions = building contractor; builder
- entrepreneur en bâtiments = building contractor

entreprise *f* enterprise; undertaking; firm; company
- entreprise de déménagement = removal firm
- entreprise privée = private company

entretenir *v* maintain (to); service (to)

entretien *m* maintenance; servicing
- frais d'entretien = maintenance cost(s)/ expenses/expenditure

enveloppe *f* jacket; casing; cover; lagging; jacketing
- enveloppe de cylindre = cylinder-jacket

épaisseur *f* thickness; depth

équipe *f* team; shift; gang
- chef d'équipe = foreman

équipement *m* fittings; fitments; fitting out
- l'équipement électrique = the electrical fittings
- l'équipement extérieur = exterior fittings
- les équipements = facilities/amenities

équiper *v* equip (to); fit (to); to install fitments
- cuisine équipée = fitted kitchen

escabeau *m* **1** step-ladder; pair of steps; **2** stool

escalier *m* stairs; staircase; stairway; steps
- escalier de dégagement = private or back staircase
- escalier en colimaçon = spiral staicase
- escalier tournant = spiral staircase

esquisse *f* sketch; rough sketch; outline (of a project)

étable *f* cowshed; cattle-shed; shed
- étable à porceaux = pigsty

établir *v* **1** establish (to); set up (to); **2** write (to) (a cheque); **3** draw up (to) (eg plans); **4** fix (to) (a price)
- établir un chèque à l'ordre de = to write a cheque to

étage *m* floor; storey; floor level
- maison à deux étages = three-storeyed house
- mezzanine étage = mezzanine; mezzanine floor
- premier/deuxième étage = first/second floor

étagère *f* shelf

étanchéité *f* waterproofness; watertightness; imperviousness; airtightness

étang *m* pond; pool

étape *f* stage; step
- étape de la construction = construction stage

état *m* state; condition
- à l'état de projet = at the planning stage
- en état = in order
- en état de marche = in working order
- état civil = marital status; family status
- état des lieux = report of state of accommodation; inventory of fixtures
- état pro forma = pro forma statement
- remettre en état = to refurbish/renovate; to recondition

éteindre *v* switch off (to) (eg lamp); turn off (to) (eg electricity); extinguish (to) (eg fire, cigarette)

éviction *f* eviction; dispossession

évier *m* sink; kitchen sink
- bloc-évier = sink unit
- évier à un bac/deux bacs = single/double sink
- évier en inox = stainless steel sink
- évier simple/double bac = sink with single/double bowl

examiner *v* examine (to); discuss (to)
- examiner la maison de plus près = to take a closer/second look at the house

excavation *f* excavation; excavating; digging

exemplaire *m* copy
- en trois exemplaires = three copies; in triplicate

expédition *f* **1** certified copy of l'acte de vente given to property buyer by notary; **2** dispatch; **3** consignment

expert *m* expert; specialist; professional
- expert en assurance = loss adjuster
- géomètre expert = surveyor
- expert immobilier = chartered surveyor; property valuer

expertise *f* expert valuation/appraisal; survey; surveyor's report
- expertise d'un bien = valuation of a property

exposé au sud/nord/est/ouest facing south/north/east/west
- maison bien exposée = well situated house
- endroit très exposé = very exposed place (eg to the wind)

extérieur *m* (also adj) exterior; outside

extrait *m* extract
- extrait (d'acte) de mariage = marriage certificate
- extrait (d'acte) de naissance = birth certificate

F

fabriquer *v* manufacture (to); fabricate (to); make (to)

façade *f* facade; front; frontage
- façade latérale = side wall
- la façade arrière de la maison = the back of the house

facture *f* **1** invoice; bill; **2** manufacture; make; workmanship

- meubles de bonne facture = well-made furniture
- régler une facture = to pay a bill

facturer *v* invoice (to)

faïence *f* earthenware (glazed)
- carreau de faïence = ceramic wall tile

faïencerie *f* earthenware factory

faubourg *m* suburb (inner)

faux-plafond *m* false ceiling; intermediate ceiling

fêler (se) *v* crack (to)

fêlure *f* crack

fenêtre *f* window
- fenêtre à guillotine = sash window
- fenêtre à tabatière = skylight
- fenêtre en saillie = bay or bow window
- fenêtre mansardée = dormer window
- fenêtre ordinaire = casement window; French window

fer *m* iron; bit (of tool)
- chemin de fer = railway
- fer à souder = soldering iron
- fer blanc = tin plate; tin plated iron sheet
- fer de fonte (ou simplement fonte) = cast iron
- fer forgé = wrought iron
- fer noir = black sheet iron

fermage *m* 1 farm rent; rent paid for use of arable land; 2 tenant farming

ferme *f* (1) farm; farmhouse
- cour de ferme = farmyard
- fermette *f* = (small) farmhouse

ferme *f* (2) roof timbers; roof truss; girder; steel roof truss

feutre *m* felt; felting
- feutrage *m* = felting

fiche *f* 1 plug (elect); jack plug; 2 record; index card; 3 hinge; hinge pin
- fiche d'état civil = record of civil status (ie birth and marriage certificates)
- fiche électrique = electric plug

fil *m* 1 wire; thread; 2 cord (of electric appliance); 3 cutting edge (of a tool); 4 grain (of wood); 5 filament (of electric bulb)
- fil sous tension = live wire (elect)
- fil de phase = live wire; live conductor
- fil neutre = neutral wire
- téléphone sans fil = cordless telephone

fleuve *m* river; major river

FNAIM; Fédération Nationale des Agents Immobiliers et Mandataires en vente de

Fonds National Federation of Estate Agents (France)

fondation *f* foundation; base
- fondations d'un batiment = foundations of a building
- fondation sur pieux/pilotis = pile foundation

fondement *m* foundation; base
- fondements d'une maison = foundations of a house

fonds *m* 1 land; estate; 2 fund(s)
- bien fonds = real estate
- fonds de terre = estate (part of); piece of land
- le fonds dominant = dominating land (of easements on other land)
- les fonds = funds; capital

fonte *f* 1 cast iron; pig iron; 2 melting; 3 casting
- fonte brute = pig iron
- fonte de fer = cast iron

forêt *f* forest
- forêt domaniale = national/state owned forest

forfait *m* fixed price or rate; contract; agreed sum; lump-sum contract
- contrat à forfait = contract at an agreed price
- prix à forfait = lump sum
- prix forfaitaire = contract price; all-inclusive price

fosse *f* 1 pit; 2 grave
- fosse d'aisances = earth closet; cesspit
- fosse septique = septic tank

fossé *m* ditch
- fossé collecteur = drainage ditch
- fossé d'irrigation = irrigation channel

fouille *f* 1 excavation; excavating; digging; excavation site; trench; 2 search

four *m* oven; furnace
- four à pain = bread oven; baker's oven
- four au micro-ondes = microwave oven
- plat allant au four = ovenproof/fireproof dish

fournisseur *m* supplier; retailer; stockist; tradesman

frais *m/mpl* charge(s); fees; cost; expenses; expenditure
- frais d'enregistrement = registration fees
- frais d'entretien = maintenance cost(s)/expenses/expenditure
- frais de déménagement = removal expenses
- frais de dossier = mortgage arrangement fee
- frais de justice = legal costs
- frais de main-d'oeuvre = labour costs
- frais en sus = additional charges/costs

fusible *m* fuse; fuse-wire
- fondre un fusible = to blow a fuse
- fusible à cartouche = cartridge fuse
- fusible principal = main fuse
- griller un fusible = to blow a fuse
- porte-fusibles *m* = fuse board; fuse box

G

galvaniser *v* galvanize (to)
- galvanisé = galvanized
- tôle galvanisée = galvanized iron sheet

gamme *f* range; gamut; scale; series
- gamme de prix = price range
- une maison haut/bas de gamme = house at the upper/lower end of the range

garage *m* garage
- garage à bicyclettes = bicycle shed

garantie *f* guarantee; security; collateral
- garantie extrinsèque = guarantee supported by financial institution
- garantie intrinsèque = guarantee unsupported by financial institution

gardien *m*; **gardienne** *f* caretaker; keeper; warden
- gardien d'immeuble = caretaker of an apartment block
- maison de gardien = caretaker's lodge/house

garrigue *f* scrubland; garrigue; scrub on hillside (Mediterranean)

gaz *m* gas
- G.D.F. = Gaz de France = French Gas Board
- gaz de ville = mains gas; town gas
- gaz en bouteille = bottled gas
- gaz propane/butane = propane/butane gas

gazier *m* gas fitter
- ajusteur-gazier = gas fitter
- plombier = plumber and gas fitter

gazon *m* grass; lawn; turf
- gazon anglais = smooth/well-kept lawn
- une motte/plaque de gazon = a turf

génie civil *m* civil engineering
- génie sanitaire = sanitary engineering

gentilhommière *f* manor house (small); (small) country house

géologue *m/f* geologist

géomètre *m* surveyor; geometrician; geometer
- géomètre expert = surveyor (land)
- levé de géomètre = survey; surveyor's report
- géomètre du cadastre = ordnance surveyor

gérant *m*; **gérante** *f* manager; manageress; managing agent
- gérant d'immeubles = managing agent of block of flats

gestion *f* management; administration
- frais de gestion = administrative expenses
- gestion immobilière = estate agency management

gestionnaire *m/f*; also *adj* administrator

gouttière *f* gutter; drainpipe

granit *m* granite

grange *f* barn

gravats *mpl*; **gravois** *m* rubble; demolition rubble

gravier *m* gravel

grenier *m* attic; loft
- grenier à foin = hayloft

grès *m* earthenware
- conduit en grès = earthenware drain

grever *v* 1 burden (to); encumber (to); 2 entail (to)

grillage *m* wire netting; wire fencing; wire mesh fencing; wiremesh

grille *f* 1 grille; grating; bars (window); 2 railings; 3 gate (metal); 4 grid (electricity)
- grille de clôture = surrounding railing

griller *v* blow (to); burn out (to) (fuse, electric motor, etc)

gros-œuvre *m* 1 basic structure; foundations and walls; outer walls; 2 shell (of a building)

H

habillage *m* 1 decorative cladding; 2 lagging (heat insulation); 3 casing (of a machine)

habitation *f* house; dwelling
- groupe d'habitations = block of flats; housing estate
- habitation principale = main residence
- immeuble d'habitation = block of flats
- taxe d'habitation = rates; community charge

habiter *v* live in (to); occupy (to)
- habiter à la campagne/en ville = to live in the country/in town

haie *f* hedge

■ haie d'aubépines = hawthorn hedge

hangar *m* shed; warehouse; lean-to; outhouse

■ hangar à récoltes = Dutch barn; open-sided barn

hauteur *f* height; elevation; altitude

■ hauteur au-dessus du niveau de la mer = height above sea-level

hectare *m*; **ha** *abb* hectare (10,000 sq. metres = 2.4711 acres)

hérisson *m* **(1)** flue brush; chimney sweep's brush

hérisson *m* **(2) 1** foundation consisting of a next-to-earth compacted layer of stones; **2** flagging laid on foundation of large stones

hérissonnage *m* laying/layer of stones forming bedding for flagstones or solid flooring

hérissonner *v* roughcast (to) (masonry)

honoraires *mpl* fee; fees

■ les honoraires de l'architecte = architect's fee

hors taxe *adj* exclusive of tax; excluding taxes; before tax; tax free

■ hors-taxe = duty free

huisserie *f* frame; door frame; window frame

huissier *m* bailiff

■ huissier de justice = bailiff

humide *adj* damp; humid; moist

hypothèque *f* mortgage

hypothèquer *v* mortgage (to); secure by mortgage (to)

■ lever/prendre une hypothèque = to raise a mortgage

I

immeuble *m* building; block of flats; real estate; premises

■ immeuble à usage locatif = block of rented flats

■ immeuble de rapport = block of flats; investment property

immobilisation *f* immobilization (of capital, etc); tied-up assets

■ indemnité d'immobilisation = type of deposit (liable to forfeit) paid on a property under 'une promesse de vente' agreement

imperméable *adj* impermeable; waterproof; drip proof

■ imperméabiliser *v* = to waterproof

■ revêtment impermeable = waterproof coating/covering

implantation *f* laying out (of ground plan); setting out; siting; locating

■ plan d'implantation de la maison sur le terrain = siting plan for house

imposte *f* **1** fanlight; **2** transom (window)

impôt *m* tax; tax liability; taxation; tax rate

■ impôt foncier = land tax; property tax

■ impôt sur le revenu = income tax

incendie *m* fire (eg accidental); conflagration; blaze

■ assurance incendie = fire insurance

indivision *f* joint possession; joint ownership

■ propriété en indivision = jointly held property (on death of one owner their share is subject to French succession law) (see also 'tontine')

ingénieur *m* engineer

■ ingénieur des eaux et fôrets = forestry expert

inoxydable *adj*; **inox** *abb* stainless

■ (acier) inox = stainless steel

installateur *m* fitter

■ installateur en chauffage central = central heating installation engineer

installation *f* installation; fitting(s); installing

■ installation(s) sanitaire(s)/électrique(s) = sanitary/electrical fittings or installations

installer *v* put in (to); install (to); fit out (to)

interdit,-e *adj* forbidden; prohibited; banned

■ interdit bancaire = withdrawal of banking facilities

■ être interdit de chéquier = to have chequebook facilities withdrawn

intérêt *m* interest

■ intérêt simple/composé = simple/compound interest

■ intérêts arriérés/arrérages = interest in arrears

■ intérêts moratoires = interest on arrears; back interest

intérieur *m*; also *adj* interior; inside

■ l'intérieur de la maison = the interior of the house

■ une cour intérieure = an inner courtyard

interlocuteur *m*; **interlocutrice** *f* **1** speaker; person; **2** negotiator; **3** representative

interrupteur *m* switch (elect); circuit-breaker

isolation *f* insulation

■ isolation thermique/phonique/acoustique = heat/sound/ acoustic insulation

■ ruban isolant *m* = insulating tape

isolateur *m* insulator
isolement *m* 1 insulation; 2 isolation

J

jambage *m* 1 jamb; jamb-post; door post; 2 foundation wall; 3 stone pier
- jambage de force = strut/prop
- jambage d'une baie de porte = jamb-post of a doorway
- jambage d'une cheminée = jamb of a fire-place

jardin *m* garden; vegetable garden; yard
- jardin d'hiver = winter garden; conservatory
- jardin de rocaille = rockery; rock garden
- jardin potager = vegetable or kitchen garden

jardinière *f* window box

joint *m* 1 joint; seal; gasket; 2 pointing (masonry)
- joint de robinet = tap washer
- joint d'étanchéité = seal

jointoyer *v* 1 point (to) (masonry); 2 grout (to)
- rejointoyer = to repoint; to regrout
- rejointoiement m = repointing; regrouting

jouissance *f* use; possession of; tenure; enjoyment
- date de jouissance = due date (of interest)
- jouissance libre = vacant possession
- multijouissance = time-share
- privation de jouissance = deprivation of use of (eg property)

L

lac *m* lake
- lac d'agrément = ornamental lake

laine *f* de verre glass-wool

laine *f* minérale; laine *f* de roche mineral wool; rock wool

laiton *m* brass
- laiton fondu = cast brass

lambris *m* panelling; cladding (decorative); lining; wainscoting; wood strip, tongued-and-grooved

lambrissage *m* panelling; wainscoting

lambrisser *v* panel (to); wainscot (to); line (to)

largeur *f* width; breadth
- largeur hors-tout = overall width

lavabo *m* washbasin
- lavabos = wash place; toilets; loo (eg in a restaurant)

lave-linge *m* washing machine

lave-vaisselle *m* dishwasher

ledit; ladite; lesdit(e)s *adj* the aforementioned; the aforesaid (in legal documents)

lézarde *f* crack; crevice; split (eg in wall)

liège *m* cork

lier *v* bind (to); fasten (to); join together (to) (eg with tie or strap)

lieudit, lieu-dit *m* locality; named place

lingerie *f* linen room

lissage *m* smoothing
- enduit de lissage = smoothing coat/plaster

lisser *v* smooth (to); smooth down (to)

listel *m* border tile (wall tile)

liteau *m* batten

livraison *f* delivery

local *m;* **locaux** *pl* premises
- local à usage commercial = shop; commercial premises
- local d'habitation = domestic premises; private dwelling
- locaux = offices; premises

local,-e *adj* local

locataire *f* tenant; renter; lessee
- locataire à bail = lessee; leaseholder
- sous-locataire = sub-lessee

location *f* renting; letting; renting out
- location avec option d'achat = leasing, or lease-option agreement
- location-bail = lease; leasing; leasehold
- location-vente = hire purchase; purchase by instalments
- location d'outillage = tool hire

loge *f* lodge; loggia; hut; cabin
- logette *f* = small lodge

logement *m* dwelling house; accommodation; apartment; flat; lodging
- logement achevé = a completed house
- logement neuf = new house/apartment

logis *m* 1 dwelling; home; residence; 2 manor house; 3 small hotel; inn; lodging-house

longère *f* long barn or house; Breton farmhouse

longueur *f* length
- longueur hors-tout = overall length

lotissement *m* 1 plot or parcel of land; 2 housing estate or site; housing development; 3 dividing up (into lots)

louer *v* rent (to)
- maison à louer = house to rent

loyer *m* rent
- loyer de l'argent = price of money; rate of interest

lu et approuvé, bon pour accord read, approved and agreed (endorsement put on a legal document, with signature)

lucarne *f* dormer window

lumière *f* light

luminaire *m* light; lamp
- luminaire extérieur = exterior light
- magasin de luminaires = lighting shop

M

maçon *m* mason; stone-mason; bricklayer; builder
- ouvrier/compagnon maçon = mason's mate

maçonner *v* face (to); brick (to); lay bricks or stone (to); brick up (to)

maçonnerie *f* masonry; brickwork; stonework; brick or stone laying; building

magasin *m* shop; store; warehouse

main-d'œuvre *f* labour; labour force or work force; manpower
- prix/coût de la main-d'œuvre = labour cost(s)

mainlevée *f* restoration of goods
- mainlevée de saisie = cancellation of garnishee order
- mainlevée d'hypothèque = release of mortgage

mainmise *f* seizure

maire *m*; **mairesse** *f* mayor; mayoress (seldom used)

mairie *f* town hall; council offices; office of mayor

maison *f* 1 house; 2 firm or company
- maison à deux étages = three-storeyed house
- maison à toit de chaume = thatched cottage (see also chaumière)
- maison bourgeoise = period house (eg built early part of 20th century)
- maison d'habitation = dwelling house/private house
- maison de campagne = cottage/house situated in the countryside
- maison de commerce = business firm
- maison de/en pierres = stone cottage/house
- maison de ferme = farmhouse
- maison de maître = architecturally superior country or town house; family mansion
- maison en ancien = old house; previously owned house
- maison en neuf = new house
- maison individuelle = detached house
- maison jumelle = semi-detached house; duplex
- maisons mitoyennes = semi-detached houses; terraced houses; house joined each side
- une maison de 5 pièces = a 5-roomed house

maisonnette *f* small house; maisonette; lodge; country cottage

maître *m* **d'œuvre** project manager
- maître d'œuvre qualifié = qualified building supervisor (eg architect, building contractor)

maître d'ouvrage *m* 1 developer; 2 owner (commissioning building work)

malfaçon *f* fault; defect (due to poor workmanship)

mandant *m*; **mandante** *f* principal

mandat *m* mandate; power of attorney; proxy
- mandat exclusif = exclusive selling order (single agent)
- mandat-poste = postal order
- mandat simple = non-exclusive selling order (two or more agents)

mandataire *m* authorised agent; representative; mandatary; assignee; proxy

manoir *m* manor; manor house; country house

mansarde *f* attic (in a mansard roof); mansard (roof)
- la chambre est mansardée = the room has a sloping ceiling
- toit/comble en mansarde = mansard roof; curb roof

marais *m* marsh; marshland; bog; swamp

marbre *m* marble

marché *m* market; bargain; deal
- faire un marché avantageux = to make a good bargain
- marché couvert/en plein air = covered/open-air market

marée _f_ tide
- à marée haute/basse = at high/low tide

marteau _m_ hammer

mas _m_ mas; stone house (traditionally built in Provence or Languedoc); small farmhouse; Mediterranean style house

masse _f_ 1 mass; 2 massive structure; 3 earth (elect)
- faire masse = act as earth
- la masse de l'édifice = massive structure of the building
- masse active/passive = assets/liabilities (legal)
- plan de masse = site plan; structural plan; massing plan

mastic _m_ putty; filler; mastic
- couteau à mastiquer = putty knife
- couteau de vitrier = glazier's knife; putty knife
- mastiquer = to putty; to fill

matériau _m_; **matériaux** _mpl_ material; materials
- matériau de revêtement = lining material
- matériaux de construction = building/construction materials

matériel _m_; **matériels** _pl_; also _adj_ equipment; plant; appliances; materials
- matériel de brasage = brazing/hard soldering equipment

mazet _m_ cottage; villa; small farmhouse; small stone hut

mazout _m_ fuel oil; heating oil
- chauffage central au mazout = oil-fired central heating

menuiserie _f_ 1 joinery; carpentry; 2 joiner's workshop; 3 piece of joinery/carpentry
- menuiserie métallique = metal joinery (eg doors, windows)

menuisier _m_ joiner; carpenter
- menuisier d'art = cabinet-maker

mer _f_ 1 sea; 2 tide
- niveau de la mer = sea level

métal _m_, **métaux** _mpl_ metal, metals

métallerie _f_ metalwork; metal grilles, metal items, etc; metal working

métrage _m_ 1 measurement; measuring; 2 metric length; 3 quantity surveying; surveying

mètre _m_ metre; metre rule
- mètre à ruban = measuring tape; tape measure
- mètre carré = square metre

- mètre cube = cubic metre

mètré _m_ quantity surveying; measurement; estimate of costs

métreur _m_; **métreuse** _f_ quantity surveyor; surveyor

meuble _adj_ movable; loose
- biens meubles = movables; personal estate
- terre meuble = loose/soft soil or ground

meuble _m_ piece of furniture
- le meuble de jardin = garden furniture
- les meubles = the furniture
- meubles de bonne facture = well-made furniture
- meubles meublant = furniture; movables

meubler _v_ furnish (to)
- appartement meublé = furnished apartment
- non-meublé = unfurnished
- pièce meublée = furnished room

miroiterie _f_ mirror industry; mirror trade; mirror items

mise _f_ putting; setting
- à la mise hors d'air = building stage with doors and windows completed
- à la mise hors d'eau = building stage with roof completed

mise _f_ **au point** 1 developing; perfecting; 2 adjustment; tuning; 3 finalising/settling (business); 4 clarification
- publier une mise au point = to issue a statement/ clarification

mise _f_ **en demeure** summons; formal demand; formal notice

mise _f_ **en œuvre** 1 implementation (eg of a regulation); 2 make use of; 3 carrying out; execution (eg of building work); 4 setting up; 5 placing (eg of concrete)

mitoyenneté _f_ common ownership (eg of a wall or fence)
- la mitoyenneté des maisons = the presence of a party wall between the houses

mobilier _m_ furniture; personal or movable property

modalité _f_ form; mode; method; modality; means; way
- modalités de mise en œuvre = details of implementation
- modalités de paiement = methods/terms of payment

modifier _v_ modify (to); alter (to)
- se modifier = to alter; to be modified

moellon *m* rubble; rubble-stone; quarry stone; small irregular shaped stone
- moellonage *m* = rubble work; ashlar work

moisissure *f* mould; mildew

montant *m* (1) amount; total amount; sum; price
- montant brut = gross amount
- montant dû/forfaitaire = outstanding amount
- montant net = net amount

montant *m* (2) riser (of staircase); upright (stile) (of door, window); post (eg of gate)

monter *v* 1 assemble (to); 2 connect (to) (electrically); wire up (to) (eg piece of equipment); 3 rise (to); mount (to)
- démonter = to take down; to dismantle

moquette *f* fitted carpet

mortier *m* mortar

moulin *m* mill
- moulin à eau = water-mill
- moulin à vent = windmill

moulure *f* moulding; trunking (elect)

multipropriété *f* time-sharing; time-share
- acheter un studio en multipropriété = to buy a time-share apartment

mur *m* wall
- mur de clôture = outer/surrounding wall
- mur en agglomérés/parpaings = block wall
- mur en pierres sèches = drystone wall/dyke
- mur mitoyen = party wall
- mur portant; mur porteur = bearing wall; load-bearing wall

muraille *f* high or thick wall
- les murailles de la ville = the town walls

murer *v* wall (to); wall up (to); brick (to); lay bricks (to)

muret *m* low wall

mutation *f* transfer (conveyance) of property; change of ownership

mutuelle *f* mutual benefit insurance company; friendly society
- payer sa cotisation à la mutuelle = to pay one's insurance contribution

N

nantissement *m* security; collateral
- nantissement du prix = purchase price guaranteed

négociation *f* negotiation

négocier *v* negotiate (to)

net, nette *adj* 1 clean; 2 free of (eg tax); 3 net (eg price, weight, etc)
- net de tout impôt = tax-free
- revenu net = net income

nettoiement *m* 1 cleaning; 2 clearing (agric)
- service du nettoiement = refuse disposal; cleansing department

nettoyage *m* cleaning; cleansing; clean-up

nettoyer *v* clean (to); scour (to); cleanse (to); clear (to)

neuf, neuve *adj* new
- à l'état neuf = as new
- remettre à neuf = to renovate; to refurbish

neutre *adj* neutral
- conducteur neutre = neutral conductor; neutral wire

niveau *m* level; storey
- hauteur au-dessus du niveau de la mer = height above sea-level
- niveau de bruit = noise level

non-conformité *f* not in accordance with; not in compliance with

notaire *m* notary; notary public; solicitor (conveyancing)

note *f* 1 account; bill; invoice; 2 note; memo
- note de l'électricité = electricity bill

noyer *m* walnut; walnut wood

nuire *v* harm (to); be injurious to (to); prejudice (to)

O

obstruction *f* stoppage; obstruction; blockage

œil-de-bœuf *m* bull's eye window; round window

œuvre *f* work; piece of work; undertaking
- second œuvre = finishing works; completion work of a construction
- œuvre gros = structural work

offre *f* offer; bid; tender

offre *f* **de prix** offer; quotation

ordre *m* association; professional association; order
- à l'ordre de = to the order of (cheque)
- ordre de vente = selling order
- Ordre des Architectes = Association of architects

- Ordre des Avocats = Association of barristers

ordures *fpl* rubbish (household); refuse; garbage
- boite à ordures *f* = rubbish bin; dustbin
- ordures ménagères = household rubbish
- ramassage d'ordures *m* = rubbish collection

orientation *f* aspect; orientation
- l'orientation du jardin à l'ouest = the garden's western aspect

orifice *m* opening; aperture; orifice
- orifice d'aération = air vent
- orifice de sortie = outlet

origine *f* origin; source
- certificat d'origine = certificate of origin
- origine de propriété = vendor's title to property

ossature *f* framework; structure
- ossature métallique = metal framework

outil *m* tool

outillage *m* tools; implements; machinery; equipment

ouvrage *m* work; building work
- ouvrage d'art = permanent structure; civil engineering structure (eg bridge)
- ouvrage de maçonnerie = masonry work
- se mettre à l'ouvrage = to start work

ouvrier *m*; **ouvrière** *f* workman; worker
- ouvrier du bâtiment = builder's labourer
- ouvrier de chantier = labourer
- ouvrier de construction = construction worker
- ouvrière = female worker (admin. or factory)

P

pacage *m* **1** pasture land; grazing land; pasturing; grazing
- droit(s) de pacage = grazing rights

paiement *m* payment
- faire un paiement = to make a payment
- paiement arriéré = overdue payment
- paiement en liquide = cash payment

pailler *m* straw yard; straw loft; barn for straw

palier *m* landing (of a staircase)
- avancer/procéder par paliers = to proceed by stages
- le même palier = the same floor
- porte palière = landing door

palissade *f* fencing; boarding

panne *f* purlin; side-timber
- panne filière = purlin

panneau *m* panel
- panneau de particules = chipboard; particle board
- panneau solaire = solar panel
- panneaux vitrés = glass panels; glass panelling

panty *m* long, small house (Brittany); fisherman's house

papier *m* **à calquer** tracing paper

papier *m* **à dessin** drawing paper

papier *m* **peint** wallpaper
- papier peint lavable et lessivable = washable wallpaper
- papier peint vinyl = vinyl wallpaper

parc *m* grounds (of a mansion or chateau); park
- parc à l'anglaise = landscaped garden or park
- parc à la française = formal garden (French style)
- parc naturel = nature reserve

parcellaire *adj* divided into plots

parcelle *f* parcel (of land)
- parcelle de terre = plot of land

parement *m* face; facing (of a building)
- parement d'un mur = face of wall

paroi *f* wall; inner/inside wall; interior surface; partition
- paroi interne = inner surface/wall

parpaing *m* perpend; bond-stone; concrete block (with air channels); breeze block
- mur en agglomérés/parpaings = breeze block wall; concrete block wall

parquet *m* parquet or wooden floor
- parqueter *v* = to lay a wooden or parquet floor

partage *m* sharing; division; allotment
- partage d'une succession = division of an estate

partager *v* divide (up) (to); share (to)

particulier *m* person; private individual

partie *f* **1** party; person signing a contract; litigant; **2** part; amount
- parties communes = common parts of property
- les parties contractantes = the contracting parties

passage *m* **1** way; passage; **2** change; changeover
- droit *m* de passage = right of way; easement
- passage interdit = no entry

- servitude *f* de passage = right of way
passation *f* **1** signing (a contract, deed); drawing up (a contract); **2** entry (into accounts ledger); **3** placing (an order)
  - passation de l'acte = signing the deed of sale
  - passation des marchés = signing business contracts
passe-partout *m* master key
passe-plats *m* serving hatch
patrimoine *m* estate; inheritance
  - gestion de patrimoine = private assets/estate management
pavillon *m* villa; house; lodge; lightly-built cottage; pavilion; wing (of a building)
  - pavillon de banlieue = house in the suburbs
  - pavillon de chasse = hunting lodge
paysage *m*; **paysager, paysagère** *adj* landscape; scenery
  - jardin paysagé = landscaped garden
  - parc paysager = landscaped garden
peindre *v* paint (to)
  - peindre les boiseries = to paint the woodwork
  - repeindre = to repaint
peintre *m/f* painter
  - peintre-décorateur = painter and decorator
  - peintre en bâtiment = house painter
peinture *f* painting; paintwork; paint
  - application de peinture à deux couches = two coats of paint
  - attention à la peinture!/peinture fraîche! = wet paint
  - peinture brillante = gloss paint
  - peinture crépi = masonry paint (textured)
  - peinture d'apprêt; peinture de fond = priming paint; primer
  - peinture emulsion = emulsion paint
  - peinture laqueé = gloss paint; enamel
  - peinture mate = matt emulsion (paint)
  - peinture satinée = satin-finish paint
  - peinture vernissante = enamel
  - rouleau à peinture = paint roller
pelle *f* shovel; spade
  - pelle à poussière = dustpan
pelouse *f* lawn; grassed area
penderie *f* wardrobe (for hanging garments only)
pente *f* slope; pitch (of roof); slant
  - en pente = sloping
  - la pente d'un toit = the pitch of a roof
percepteur *m* tax-collector
perception *f* **1** tax-collector's office;

2 collection; levy; charge
permis *m* **de construire** planning permission; building permit (usually issued from local mayor's office)
permis *m* **de démolir** permit to demolish a building
perron *m* steps (leading to an entrance); covered porch reached by an outside staircase; front steps (of a house)
persiennes *fpl* louvred or slatted shutters (S. France)
phase *f* phase; live wire (elect)
pièce *f* room (of house)
  - appartement de 5-pièces = 5-roomed flat
  - pièce haute (basse) de plafond = high (low)-ceilinged room
  - pièce principale = main room
  - un deux-pièces cuisine = a 2-roomed flat with kitchen
pied-à-terre *m* small flat in town; temporary quarters; pied-à-terre
pierre *f* stone
  - maison de/en pierre = stone-built house
  - pierre de taille = freestone; ashlar; building-stone
  - pierre du pays = local stone
pieu *m* **1** pile (constr); **2** post; stake;
pigeonnier *m* pigeon house or loft; dovecot
pignon *m* gable
  - à pignon = gabled
pinceau *m* paintbrush (see brosse)
piquet *m* post; stake; picket
  - piquet de clôture = fence post
  - piquet de terre = earthing rod (elect)
piscine *f* swimming pool
placage *m* veneer; veneering
placard *m* cupboard
  - placard à balai = broom cupboard
  - placard de cuisine = kitchen cupboard
plafond *m* ceiling
  - faux-plafond = false ceiling
  - plafond lambrissé = panelled or boarded ceiling
  - plafond voûté = vaulted/arched ceiling
plan *m* **1** plan; blueprint; scale drawing; map; **2** project; **3** plane
  - acheter une maison sur plan = to buy a house at the planning stage
  - dresser les plans de = to make plans for (a house, garden)

- plan de construction = construction plan or drawing
- plan de la coupe transversale = cross-sectional plan
- plan de la façade = elevation plan (eg front, side, rear)
- plan de la maison = house plan
- plan de masse; plan-masse = location of building on site plan; aerial plan of mass; massing plan
- plan de situation du terrain = drawing / plan of cadastral situation of site
- plan d'implantation = layout plan of building on a site
- Plan d'Occupation des Sols = plan of land occupancy (officially published plan showing development zones etc)
- plan étage = plan of upper floor
- plan rez = plan of ground floor
- tirer des plans = to draw up plans

planche *f* 1 board; floorboard; plank; 2 shelf
- planche à dessin = drawing board
- planche voilée = warped board
- planchette *f* = small shelf

plancher *m* floor; flooring

plaque *f* sheet; plate; slab; cover
- plaque d'égout = manhole cover
- plaque de plâtre = plasterboard (sheet)
- plaque de propreté = fingerplate

plaquer *v* veneer (to); plate (to) (with metal)

plâtre *m* plaster
- panneau/plaque de plâtre = plasterboard
- placoplâtre = plasterboard (TM)
- plâtrage *m* = plastering; setting in plaster

plâtrer *v* plaster (to); render (to)

plâtrier *m* plasterer

plinthe *f* skirting board; skirting; plinth (of column); base-board

plomb *m* 1 lead (metal); 2 plumbline; plumb; plumb-bob
- la maison se tient à plomb = the house stands plumb

plomberie *f* plumbing; plumber's workshop; leadwork

plombier *m* plumber

plus-value *f* increase in value; appreciation; gain in value
- impôt sur les plus-values = capital gains tax

point *m* point; place; dot
- point de congélation = freezing point

pointe *f* point; tip; brad; nail
- clou à deux pointes (agrafe *f*) = staple; wire-staple
- pointe d'un clou = point of a nail
- pointe tête plate = flat-headed nail; wire nail

police *f* policy (insurance)
- police d'assurance contre l'incendie = fire insurance policy
- police multirisques habitation = comprehensive building insurance policy

pompe *f* pump
- pompe de circulation = circulating pump
- pompe électrique = electric pump

ponçage *m* rubbing down; sanding (down); sandpapering; pumicing

poncer *v* rub down (to); sand or sand down (to); sandpaper (to)

ponceuse *f* sander; sanding machine
- ponceuse orbitale = orbital sander
- ponceuse à bande = belt sander
- ponceuse à parquet = floor sander

pont *m* bridge
- les Ponts et Chaussées = the highways department; civil engineering department

porche *m* porch; porchway

porcherie *f* pigsty

portail *m* portal; front entrance *(archit)*; gate; *(pl)* double gates
- portail metallique = metal gate

porte *f* door; doorway; doorstep; gate
- porte à claire-voie = glazed door; lattice gate; barred gate
- porte à deux battants = double door or gate
- porte coulissante/pliante = sliding/folding door
- porte d'entrée = front door; entrance
- porte de derrière = back door
- porte-fenêtre *f* = french window
- porte palière = landing door; door opening on to landing
- porte vitrée = glass panelled door; glazed door

porter *v* carry (to); support (to); bear (a load) (to)
- porter à faux = to be out of plumb/true
- porter sur = to be supported by/on; to bear on

poser *v* install (to); fit (to); lay (to); put in (to) (eg pane of glass)

potager *m* kitchen garden; vegetable garden

poteau *m* post; pole

- poteau de bornage = boundary post
- poteau d'huisserie = jamb-post; door post
- poteau télégraphique = telegraph pole/post
poubelle *f* dustbin; rubbish bin
- boîte à ordures *f* = dustbin
poussière *f* dust
poutrage *m*; **poutraison** *f* girderage; framework of beams
poutre *f* beam; girder (metal); balk (of timber)
- poutre en béton armé = reinforced concrete beam
- poutrelle *f* = small beam or girder
- poutres apparentes = exposed beams
pouvoir *m* power; ability
- avoir pleins pouvoirs = to be fully authorised
prairie *f* meadow; grassland
pré *m* meadow; small meadow
préalable *adj* prior; previous; preliminary
préalable *m* prerequisite; condition; preliminary
préavis *m* prior notice; advance notice (given before a contract is broken)
préciser *v* specify (to); make clear (to); give precise details (to); stipulate (to)
prélèvement *m* deduction; debit; debiting; levy; charge (commission)
- ordre de prélèvement = standing order (bank)
- prélèvement automatique = direct debit
- prélèvement forfaitaire = standard deduction of tax
- prélèvement libératoire = witholding of tax with full discharge
prescription *f* 1 prescription; specifications 2 regulations; 3 statute of limitations
- les prescriptions = regulations; instructions
- les prescriptions techniques = building regulations; specifications
prestation *f* 1 provision; contribution; benefits; allowance; 2 service
- les prestations = services
- prestation de service = provision of a service
- prestation en nature = payment or benefit in kind; service charge
- prestation familiales = family benefits (paid by State)
prêt *m* loan; advance
- prêt à la construction = building loan
- prêt bancaire = bank loan
- prêt relais = bridging loan
prime d'assurance *f* insurance premium
prise *f* 1 inlet; intake; 2 hold; 3 point (elect); socket
- prise d'air = air inlet/intake
- prise d'eau = hydrant; (bouche d'incendie = fire hydrant)
- prise de courant (mâle/femelle)= electric plug/socket; power point
- prise multiple = adaptor plug
- prise pour résoir électrique = razor point
prix *m* price
- prix à forfait = lump sum price; inclusive price
- prix acte en main = total cost to buyer up to receipt of conveyance document (excluding mortgage costs)
- prix au comptant = cash price
- prix comission compris = price including agent's commission
- prix d'achat = purchase/cost price
- prix de départ = asking price
- prix demandé au départ = asking price
- prix de revient = cost price
- prix de vente = selling price
- prix forfaitaire = contract price; all-inclusive price
- prix net vendeur = net sum received by vendor
procès-verbal *m*; **procès-verbaux** *mpl* report or statement; minutes
- faire un procès-verbal = to draw up a report
procuration *f* power of attorney; proxy
- lettre de procuration = power of attorney
profondeur *f* depth
projet *m* project; plan; scheme; draft
- établir un projet d'accord/de contrat = to produce a draft agreement/contract.
- projet d'acte = draft conveyance document
projeter *v* plan (to); consider (to); project (to)
- projeter de faire quelque chose= to plan to do something
promesse *f* de vente unilateral agreement to sell; preliminary contract to sell
- promesse bilatérale = bilateral agreement to sell/buy
- promesse synallagmatique = bilateral agreement to sell/buy
promoteur *m* immobilier property developer
propriétaire *m* owner; proprietor; landlord
propriété *f* 1 property; estate; 2 ownership; possession; 3 property; characteristic
- la nouvelle propriété = sale and leaseback

property
- propriété fonciére = real estate; freehold

prorogation *f* **1** extension of time; extension of payment period; **2** renewal (of a loan)
- prorogation d'un prêt = renewal/extension of a loan

publicité *f* foncière land registration; public record of property ownership, mortgages, etc.

puits *m* well; shaft
- puits artésien = artesian well
- puits d'aération= ventilation shaft
- puits perdu = cesspool; soak away; sink
- puits profond = deep well

purgeur *m* trap; drain-cock; bleed-tap (of radiator)

Q

quartier *m* district; area; quarter; neighbourhood
- les beaux quartiers = the fashionable districts
- le quartier ouest de la ville = the west side of the town
- les gens du quartier = the local people
- quartier commerçant = shopping area
- quartier résidentiel = residential area

quincaillerie *f* **1** ironmongery; hardware; **2** ironmonger's (shop)

quittance *f* discharge; receipt
- quittance de loyer = rent receipt

quote-part *f* contribution; quota; share; individual or proportional share in a contribution/acquisition

quotité *f* quota; proportion; share; amount

R

raccordement *m* connecting; joining
- raccordement au réseau (téléphonique) = connecting the telephone
- raccordement aux égouts = connecting to the drains

radiation *f* striking off (eg from list); striking out; dismissal
- radiation d'une inscription hypothécaire = entry of a satisfaction of mortgage

ragréer *v* clean down (brickwork) (to); smooth (to); finish off (to); restore (to)
- ragrément *m* = finishing off; smoothing; cleaning down

ramonage *m* cleaning/sweeping a chimney or flue

ramoneur *m* chimney sweep

rangement(s) *m(pl)* storage space

rapport *m* **d'expertise** survey report

ravalement *m* **1** resurfacing (eg of a facade); restoration; rendering; **2** redressing (stonework); **3** coat of rough-cast or plaster; **4** cutting back (agric); trimming

rebord *m* **1** edge; rim; **2** edge-plate (of lock)
- le rebord de la cheminée = the mantelpiece or mantelshelf
- le rebord de la fenêtre = windowsill; window-ledge

réception *f* reception; receipt; acceptance
- réception des ouvrages/travaux = final verification and acceptance that building work has been satisfactorily completed to specification

rechercher *v* seek (to); hunt for (to); research (to); look for (to)
- la recherche d'une appartement = flat hunting

recoin *m* recess; nook

reconduction *f* renewal
- reconduction tacite = renewal (of lease) by tacit agreement

reçu *m* receipt

rédaction *f* wording; drafting (of a document); drawing-up
- rédaction de bail = drawing-up a lease

redevance *f* rent; rental charge (eg telephone); licence fee (eg television); dues
- redevance emphytéotique = ground rent
- redevance foncière = ground rent
- redevance ordures ménagères = domestic waste (removal) charge

rédiger *v* write (to); word (to); draft (to) (a document); draw up (to) (a contract); make out (to) (a cheque)

reduit *m* box room; tiny room; cubbyhole; retreat; nook

refaire *v* redo (to); redecorate (to); repaint (to); restore (to); refurbish (to)

réfection *f* restoration; rebuilding; repairing

réfrigérateur *m* refrigerator
- frigo = fridge; refrigerator

regard *m* man-hole; peephole; inspection hole/ window

règlement *m* 1 regulation(s); 2 settlement; payment (eg of an invoice)
- règlement intégral = payment in full
- règlement intérieur = rules and regulations; bye-laws
- règlement par chèque = payment by cheque

réglementation *f* regulation(s); control
- réglementation des changes = exchange controls
- réglementation en vigueur = regulation(s) in force

régler *v* adjust (to); regulate (to); settle (to) (a bill, a problem)
- non réglé = outstanding, unpaid
- régler une facture = to pay a bill
- régler une succession = to settle an estate

relevé *m* statement; bill; reading (of meter)
- relevé bancaire = bank account statement
- relevé de compte = account statement
- relevé de gaz/de téléphone = gas/ telephone bill
- relevé d'identité bancaire = bank account number; bank account details
- relevé du compteur = meter reading

remettre *v* 1 replace (to); 2 postpone (to); 3 remit (to) (funds); 4 deliver (to); hand over (to); 5 restart (to) (a machine)
- remettre à neuf = to refurbish
- remettre en état = to recondition; to refurbish
- remettre le moteur en marche = to start the engine again
- remettre un rendez-vous à mardi = to postpone an appointment until Tuesday

remise *f* [see also remettre] 1 delivery; handing over; 2 postponement; 3 discount; 4 shed
- remise à neuf = restoration; renovation
- remise en état = reconditioning; restoration; refurbishment

remplacer *v* replace (to)

renoncer *v* give up (to); renounce (to); abandon (to)

rénovation *f* renovation; modernisation; restoration; redevelopment

rénover *v* renovate (to); modernise (to); restore (to) (a building)
- maison rénovée = renovated house

renseignement *m* information; details; particular(s)
- demande de renseignements = request for information/details

rente *f* income; annuity; pension; rent
- rente foncière = ground rent; land rent

réparation *f* repairing; restoring; mending

réparer *v* repair (to); mend (to)

répartition *f* distribution; sharing out; allocation
- mode de répartition du partage des honoraires = way the fees are allocated

réseau *m* network; system; grid
- réseau communal d'assainissement = communal sewerage system
- réseau d'alimentation = supply system
- réseau d'éclairage = lighting system
- réseau de distribution = distribution network; ductwork
- réseau primaire en boucle = ring-main (elect)

réserve *f* reserve; stock (merchandise)
- sous réserve de modification = subject to alteration
- sous réserve que = provided that

réservoir *m* reservoir; tank; fishpond
- réservoir d'eau = water tank; cistern; water butt

résidence *f* residence; residential flats (block of)
- résidence principale = main home
- résidence secondaire = second home; holiday home

résiliation *f* termination; rescinding; cancellation
- résiliation d'un contrat = cancellation of a contract
- résiliation du bail = termination of a lease

restauration *f* restoration

restaurer *v* restore (to)
- un bâtiment restauré = a restored building

revêtement *m* coating; covering; cladding; facing; surface
- revêtement des tubes = pipe wrapping
- revêtement du sol = flooring; floor covering
- revêtement enduit = lining
- revêtement mural = wall covering;
- revêtement mural imitation carrelage = imitation tile wall covering

rez-de-chaussée *m*; **rdc** *abb* 1 ground floor; street level; 2 ground floor flat
- rez-de-jardin *m* = garden level

riverain,-e *adj* lakeside; riverside; riparian

riverain, e *m.f* lakeside resident; riverside

resident; street resident
- interdit sauf aux riverains = 'residents only'

rivière *f* river; stream

robinet *m* tap
- robinet à flotteur = ballcock
- robinet d'arrêt = stopcock
- robinet de fermature = stopcock
- robinet mélangeur/mitigeur = mixer tap
- robinet purgeur = drain-cock

robinetterie *f* taps and fittings; plumbing; tap trade

rôle *m* **d'impôt** tax list; tax roll

rompre *v* break off (to) (a contract)

rondelle *f* washer
- rondelle de robinet = tap washer

rouille *f* rust
- antirouille *adj* = anti-rust
- peinture antirouille = anti-rust/anti-corosion paint
- traitement antirouille = rustproofing

route *f* road; roadway; way; route
- route nationale/départementale = main/ secondary road
- route non goudronnée = unmade road; unmetalled road

rue *f* street
- rue piétonnière ou piétonne = pedestrianised street

ruisseau *m* **1** stream; riverlet; brook; **2** gutter (road)

S

sablage *m* sandblasting; sanding

sable *m* sand
- sable *adj* = sand-coloured
- sable liant/mordant = sharp sand
- sable à bâtir = building sand
- sablière *f* = sand-pit; sand quarry; (also ground plate of timber frame panel)

sabler *v* **1** sand (to); **2** sand or gravel a path (to); **3** sandblast (to)

S.A.F.E.R.; (Société d'Aménagement Foncier et d'Établissement Rural) *f* French Land Commission

saillie *f* ledge; projection
- en saillie = projecting; surface mounted

saisie *f* distraint; foreclosure; seizure (court order

permitting seizure of a debtor's property to force him or her to meet their obligations)

salle *f* room; hall (of a chateau)
- salle à manger = dining room
- salle d'eau = shower room
- salle de bain = bathroom
- salle de douche = shower room
- salle de séjour = living room

salon *m* **1** living room; lounge; sitting room; **2** lounge suite (furniture)
- salon de jardin = set of garden furniture
- salon de trois pièces = three-piece suite (furniture)

sanitaire *adj* sanitary

sanitaire *m* bathroom installations
- l'appareil sanitaire = bathroom appliance
- les sanitaires = bathroom/bathroom suite/bathroom plumbing
- l'installation sanitaire = bathroom plumbing

sceller *v* embed (to); seal (to); grout in (to); mortar in (to)

scie *f* saw

schéma *m*; **schème** *m* diagram; plan; scheme; sketch
- schéma de câblage = wiring diagram; circuit diagram

scierie *f* sawmill

seau *m* pail; bucket; pailful; bucketful

séchoir *m* drier; drying room; clothes drying rack
- séchoir à linge = clothes horse/rack
- séchoir à tambour = tumble-drier

secteur *m* sector; local electricity supply area
- branchement sur le secteur = connection to the local electricity supply
- le secteur = mains supply (elect)

séjour *m* **1** living room; lounge; **2** stay; sojourn; **3** dwelling place
- permis de séjour = residence permit
- séjour double = through-lounge; living room

semelle *f* footing; base-plate; wall-plate

séquestre *m* **1** receiver; trustee; stakeholder; depositary; sequestrator; **2** sequestration
- compte séquestre = stakeholder account

serre *f* greenhouse; glasshouse; conservatory (attached to house)

serrure *f* lock
- serrurier *m* = locksmith

service *m* service
- service après-vente = after-sales sevice
- service des eaux = water supply

servitude *f* easement; encumbrance; charge; *(pl)* constraint
- immeuble sans servitudes ni hypothèques = estate free from encumbrances
- les servitudes privées grevant le terrain = private easements attached to the land/site
- servitude de passage = right of way

seuil *m* sill; door sill; doorstep; doorway; threshold

siège *m* **1** seat; **2** head office; headquarters (of company)
- siège de cabinet = toilet seat

signalétique *adj* descriptive; identifying
- fiche signalétique = identification sheet/descriptive return

signature *f* signature; signing

signer *v* sign (to)

sinistre *m* accident; accidental blaze; disaster
- déclarer le sinistre = to notify an accident (for insurance)
- déterminer l'étendue du sinistre = to assess the extent of the damage

socle *m* **1** plinth; pedestal; **2** bed-plate; stand; mounting base; **3** socket outlet (elect)
- socle de prise (de courant) = socket outlet
- socle en béton = concrete base

sol *m* **1** ground; ground floor; **2** floor; flooring; **3** soil; earth; **4** earth; ground (elect)
- au sol = earthed (elect)
- la pose des sols = laying floors/flooring
- sol argileux/glaiseux = clay soil
- sol carrelé/cimenté = tiled/concrete floor
- sol en béton = concrete floor; concrete base

solde *m* **1** balance; **2** surplus stock; sale goods; sale
- solde d'un compte = balance of an account
- solde dû = balance due

solin *m* **1** fillet-gutter; **2** flashing between wall and abutting roof; **3** spacing between joists; coating of fill-in material (eg plaster)

solivage *m* joisting; girderage

solive *f* joist; beam; girder
- solive de plancher = floor joist
- solive en acier = steel joist

somme *f* sum; amount (money)
- somme à payer = amount to pay
- somme forfaiture = lump sum

sonnerie *f* bell; chimes; ringing
- sonnerie au portail = door/gate bell

- sonnerie d'alarme = alarm bell

souche *f* chimney stack (above roof level)

souillarde *f* **1** scullery; **2** hole for rainwater pipe

source *f* spring (water); source
- eau de source = spring water
- source de lumière = light source

sous-couche *f* undercoat (eg paint)

sous-œuvre *m* underpinning; substruction
- reprendre en sous-œuvre = to underpin; to shore up; to alter fundamentally; to alter groundwork of; to recast
- reprise en sous-œuvre = underpinning

soussigné *m*; **soussignée** *f*; also *adj* undersigned (the)

sous-sol *m* **1** basement; lower ground floor (of shop); **2** subsoil; substratum

souterrain *m*; also *adj* underground; subterranean (passage)

spécification *f* specification

standing *m* standing (situation and condition)
- immeuble de grand standing = block of luxury apartments
- quartier de grand standing = select district; desirable residential district

stipulation *f* stipulation; item in contract; specified item
- stipulations d'un contrat = specifications of a contract

store *m* blind; shade; awning; sun-blind
- store à lamelles orientables = Venetian blind
- store à rouleaux = roller blind
- store vénitien = Venetian blind

studio *m*; **studette** *f* studio apartment; one-room flat

succession *f* succession; inheritance; estate
- droits de succession = estate duties; death duties

superficie *f* surface; surface area
- la superficie de plancher hors œuvre nette = overall net floor area (gross area less attic, balcony, parking etc)

surestimer *v* overestimate (to); overvalue (to)
- surestimer une masison à vendre = to overvalue a house for sale

surface *f* surface; surface area; (see also 'superficie')
- faire/refaire surface = to surface/to resurface
- surface habitable = habitable surface area of dwelling (generally excludes balcony, terrace,

store room etc)
- surface hors œuvre brute = total area of all floor levels of house
- surface hors œuvre nette = basic area of house; habitable floor area

suspensif, suspensive *adj* suspensive
- condition suspensive = suspensive or let-out clause in a contract

syndic *m* syndic; legal representative of person/company; trustee; receiver
- syndic d'immeuble = managing agent (eg of block of flats)

syndicat *m* trade union; association
- syndicat de propriétaires = association of property owners; householders' association

T

taille *f* size; height (person)

tailler *v* cut (to) (stone); carve (to) (wood); trim (to) (a hedge)
- tailleur de pierre *m* = stonecutter; stonemason

taillis *m* copse; coppice; thicket; brushwood

talon *m* 1 counterfoil; slip; 2 stub; 3 heel
- talon de paiement = payment counterfoil/ slip/stub
- talon d'un chèque = cheque stub/ counterfoil

tapisser *v* wallpaper (to); line (to); cover (to)
- table à tapisser = wallpaper pasting table

tapisserie *f* 1 wall-paper; wall covering; 2 tapestry; 3 upholstery
- tapissier *m* = upholsterer; interior decorator

taux *m* rate; ratio; percentage; proportion
- taux d'intérêt = interest rate
- taux de base bancaire = base rate; base lending rate; bank rate
- taux de prêt = lending rate

taxe *f* tax; duty
- taxe à/sur la valeur ajoutée; (TVA) = value added tax ;VAT
- taxe d'habitation = habitation tax
- taxe de publicité foncière = land registration/recording tax
- taxe foncière = land tax; property tax
- toutes taxes comprises; TTC; T.T.C.; = all taxes included

terrain *m* land; plot (of land); piece of land; building land/site; ground; terrain

- terrain à bâtir = building land/site
- terrain boisé = wooded land
- terrain clos = enclosed land
- terrain constructible = land on which technically and legally one can build
- terrain entièrement viabilisé = site fully serviced
- terrain viabilisé = site with services laid on

terrasse *f* 1 terrace; 2 excavation work
- faire de la terrasse = to do excavation work
- terrasse couverte = covered terrace
- terrasse vitrée = veranda (glazed)
- toiture en terrasse = flat roof

terrassement *m* earthwork(s); embankment; excavation
- engine de terrassement = earth- moving/ excavating machine
- terrassements = groundwork; excavation
- travaux de terrassement = earthworks; excavation

terre *f* 1 ground; land; earth; soil; 2 earth (elect)
- terre argileuse = clayey soil
- terre calcaire = chalky soil
- terre sableuse = sandy soil

testament *m* will

textile mural *m* wall textile; wall covering

thermoplongeur *m* immersion heater

toit *m* roof
- armature à toit *f* = roof truss/trussing
- avant-toit *m* = eave

toiture *f* roofing; roof

tôle *f* sheet; plate; iron or steel sheet; sheet metal
- tôle de cuivre = sheet copper
- tôle ondulée = corrugated sheet metal
- tôle zinguée = galvanised iron sheet

tôlerie *f* sheet-metal workshop; metal panel workshop (auto)

tontine *f* tontine
- clause tontine = survivorship clause (on death of a joint property owner their share passes to other owner(s))

torchis *m* cob; wattle and daub (note: cob is a composition of clay, gravel and straw used for building walls; wattle and daub is interlaced twigs and sticks plastered with mud or clay to form a wall)

tournevis *m* screwdriver

traduction *f* translation; translating
- traduction en anglais = translation in English

traduire *v* translate (to)

transcription *f* **1** registration (eg of a divorce); copy (of decree etc); **2** transcription

transformer *v* transform (to); change (to); alter (to)

trappe *f* trap door; hatch; flap
- trappe accès combles = trap door access to attic/loft

travailleur *m* ; **travailleuse** *f* worker
- travailleur agricole = farm-hand; farm worker
- travailleur indépendant = self-employed worker

travaux *mpl* building works

triplex *m* apartment on three levels

trop-plein *m* overflow (pipe)
- le trop-plein d'un lavabo = the overflow of a washbasin

trou *m* hole
- trou d'homme = manhole
- trou de regard = inspection hole
- trou de serrure = keyhole

truelle *f* trowel

TTC; T.T.C; toutes taxes comprises *fpl* inclusive of tax; all taxes included

tube *m* tube; tubing; pipe
- tube d'égout = soil pipe

tuile *f* tile; roof tile
- tuile creuse/romaine/ronde = curved tile
- tuile faîtière = ridge tile
- tuile romaine = Roman tile

tutelle *f* guardianship; wardship

tuyau *m* pipe; piping; tube; hose; conduit; flue
- poseur de tuyaux = pipe fitter
- tuyau d'alimentation = supply pipe;feeder pipe
- tuyau d'arrosage = hosepipe
- tuyau d'écoulement = drain pipe
- tuyau d'égout = soil pipe
- tuyau de descente = downpipe
- tuyau de trop-plein = overflow pipe
- tuyau en caoutchouc = rubber tubing
- tuyau en cuivre = copper pipe/piping
- tuyau en plastique = plastic pipe
- tuyau en terre/en grès = earthenware pipe

tuyauterie *f* piping; pipes; tubing; pipes and fittings; pipework installation
- tuyauterie des eaux usées = waste water piping/sewers

tuyauteur *m* pipe fitter

T3, F3 see **villa**

UVW

urbanisme *m* town planning
- certificat d'urbanisme = certificate showing planning status
- disposition d'urbanisme = planning provision; planning requirement

vaisselier *m* dresser (cupboard)

valeur *f* value; worth; cost; price
- taxe sur la valeur ajoutée TVA *f* = value added tax; VAT

vasque *f* washbasin (bathroom)

vendeur *m* vendor; seller

vendre *v* **aux enchères** sell by auction (to)

vente *f* sale
- bureau de vente = sales office
- promesse de vente = preliminary sale agreement
- vente à l'amiable = sale by private treaty
- vente aux enchères = sale by auction
- vente en l'état futur d'achèvement en plan = sale "on plan"
- vente en plan = sale "on plan"
- vente en viager = sale with life interest (life annuity)
- vente immobilière = property sale

ventilateur *m* ventilator; fan
- ventilateur electrique = electric fan
- ventilateur extracteur = extractor fan

ventilation *f* **mécanique controlée; V.M.C.**; VMC mechanically controlled ventilation

verger *m* orchard

vermoulu,-e *adj* worm-eaten

vermoulure *f* woodworm hole; woodworm dust
- vermoulures = worm holes

verrou *m* bolt; door bolt
- verrou de porte = door-bolt

versement *m* payment; instalment; settlement; remittance
- bordereau de versement = paying-in slip (bank)
- par versements échelonnés = by instalments
- versement par chèque/virement = payment by cheque/credit transfer

verser *v* pay (to); deposit money (to); remit (to); settle (to)
- verser des arrhes = to put down a deposit

vestibule *m* hall

viabilisé,-e *adj* with services; serviced
- entièrement viabilisé = fully serviced
- terrain viabilisé = land/site with services laid on

viabilité *f* practicability; basic work required on building site (eg roads, electricity, gas, water, drains and sewers)
- terrain avec/sans viabilité = land with/ without services laid on

viager *m*; also *adj* 1 life annuity; 2 life; for life *adj*
- achat en viager = purchase made against a life annuity
- mettre/acheter un bien en viager = to sell or buy a property in return for a life annuity

vice *m* fault; defect; flaw
- vice caché = latent or hidden fault/defect
- vice de construction = construction fault/defect
- vice de forme = legal flaw or irregularity

vidanger *v* empty (to); empty out (to); drain off (to) (water, oil)

vide *m*; also *adj* 1 empty space; gap; void (archit); 2 vacuum; 3 empty *adj*
- vide d'une vis = groove of a screw
- vide-sanitaire = underfloor space
- vide sous plafond = ceiling void

vider *v* empty (to); clear (to); drain (to)

vignoble *m* vineyard

villa *f* villa; modern house; cottage
- villa (T2, T3, F3) = house with 2, 3 rooms, kitchen and bathroom

village *m* village

ville *f* town; city

virement *m* transfer; credit transfer
- faire un virement d'un compte sur un autre = to make a transfer from one account to another
- virement bancaire = bank credit transfer

viticulture *f* vine-growing; viticulture

vitrage *m* glazing; windows *(pl)*; glass partition; glass door
- double vitrage = double glazing

vitre *f* window pane; pane of glass
- cloison vitrée = glass partition
- poser une vitre = to put in a window pane

vitrerie *f* glazing; glaziery; glass items

vitrier *m* glazier
- couteau à mastiquer = putty knife
- couteau de vitrier *m* = glazier's/putty knife

- mastic de vitrier *m* = putty; glaziers' putty

voie *f* lane; way

voile *f* concrete wall; shell (of building)

voiler *v* warp (to) (wood); buckle (to) (metal); veil (to); screen (to); conceal (to)

voirie *f* 1 highway system; highways management; 2 refuse collection; rubbish dump

voisinage *m* neighbourhood; vicinity; proximity

volet *m* shutter
- volet d'aération = louvre; air damper
- volet coulissant/roulant = roller shutter

voûte *f* vault; archway
- plafond voûté = vaulted/arched ceiling

WC *m* WC, water-closet; loo
- abattant (de WC) = toilet seat and cover
- cuvette de WC = WC basin/pan
- les cabinets = toilets; WCs
- siège de cabinet = toilet seat

XYZ

xylophéne *m* a wood preservative

zinc *m* zinc

zinguer *v* cover a roof with zinc (to)
- tôle zinguée = galvanized iron sheet

ENGLISH-FRENCH
(‡ see French section for examples of usage)

A

abandon (to) renoncer *v*‡
abatement dégrèvement ‡ *m*
acceptance réception *f*
accident sinistre ‡ *m*
accidental blaze incendie *m*; sinistre ‡ *m*
accommodation logement ‡ *m*
account compte ‡ *m*; note ‡ *f*
accountancy comptabilité *f*
accountant comptable *m/f*
acknowledgement of receipt (of letter, etc) accusé *m* de réception
acquire (to) acquérir *v*; acheter *v*
acquisition acquisition *f*
additional clause avenant *m*
address adresse ‡ *f*
adjust (to) régler *v*
adjustment mise *f* au point
administration gestion ‡ *f*
administrative gestionnaire *adj*
administrative order or decree arrêté ‡ *m*
administrator gestionnaire *m/f*; curateur *m*; curatrice *f*
advance (loan) prêt ‡ *m*
advance notice (before a contract is broken) préavis *m*
advocate avocat *m*; avocate *f*
agency agence ‡ *f*
agglomerate block (eg breeze block, concrete block) aggloméré *m*; agglo (*abb*)
agglomeration agglomération *f*
agreed sum forfait ‡ *m*
agreement contrat *m*; engagement *m*
air brick bouche *f* d'aération
air conditioning climatisation *f*
air gap (cavity wall) couche *f* d'air
air inlet bouche *f* d'aération
air vent bouche *f* de ventilation
align (to) aligner *v*
alignment alignement *m*
allocation répartition *f*
allotment partage *m*
allowance abattement *m*; déduction *f*
alter (to) modifier *v*; transformer *v*
altitude hauteur *f*
aluminium aluminium *m*
amendment (to a contract) avenant *m*
amicable amiable *adj*

amount somme *f*; montant *m*; quotité *f*; partie *f*
ancient ancien, ancienne *adj*; ancien *m*
annexe (extension to a building) annexe *f*
annuity rente *f*
apartment appartement ‡ *m*; logement *m*
apartment on three levels triplex *m*
apartment on two levels duplex *m*
aperture orifice *m*
apple orchard clos *m* de pommiers
appraisal bilan ‡ *m*
architect architecte *m*
archway voûte *f*
area aire *f*
area (town) quartier *m*
area of ground (appropriated, acquired or occupied) emprise *f* au sol
article clause ‡ *f*
artisan artisan *m*
asking price prix *m* de départ
aspect (orientation) orientation *f*
asphalt (bitumen) bitume *m*; asphalte *m*
assemble (to) assembler *v*; monter *v*
assessment bilan *m*
assessor's/valuer's/surveyor's report expertise *f*
asset(s) avoir *m*
assign, assignee ayant droit *m*; ayants droit *pl*; ayant cause *m*; mandataire *m*
assignee ayant droit *m*; ayants droit *pl*; ayant cause *m*; mandataire *m*
association syndicat *m*
association (professional) ordre *f*
assurance assurance *f*
attic grenier *m*; les combles *mpl*
attic (in a mansard roof) mansarde *f*
audit apurement *m*; audit *m*
authorised agent or representative mandataire *m*; syndic *m*
authority droit *m*
awning store *m*
axle arbre ‡ *m*

B

back arrière ‡ *m*
back rent loyer *m* arriéré
back-door porte *f* de derrière
backyard arrière-cour *f*
bail bond caution *f*

bailiff huissier *m*
balance due solde dû *m*
balance sheet bilan [+] *m*
balcony balcon *m*
balk (of timber) poutre *f*
bank account details relevé *m* d'identité bancaire (R.I.B.)
bargain/deal marché *m*
barn grange *f*
barrister avocat *m*; avocate *f*
bars (window) grille *f*
base fondation *f*; fondement *m*
base-board plinthe *f*
base-plate semelle *f*
basement sous-sol *m*
basement (cellar) cave *m*
basic area of house (habitable floor area) surface *f* hors œuvre nette
basic structure gros œuvre *m*
basin (bathroom) lavabo *m*; vasque *f*
bath; bathtub baignoire *f*
bathroom installations sanitaire [+] *m*
batten liteau *m*
bay baie *f*
be injurious to (to) nuire *v*
beam poutre [+] *f*
beam or girder, small poutrelle *f*
beam, exposed poutre apparente *f*
beam, reinforced concrete poutre *f* en béton armé
bear (a load) (to) porter *v*
bearing wall; load-bearing wall mur *m* portant; mur *m* porteur
bed-plate socle *m*
bedroom chambre *f*
bell sonnerie [+] *f*
beneficiary ayant droit *m*; ayants droit *pl*; ayant cause *m*
benefits prestation [+] *f*
bid enchère [+] *f*; offre *f*
bilateral agreement to sell/buy; preliminary contract to sell or buy compromis *m* de vente; promesse *f* bilatérale
bilateral contract contrat *m* synallagmatique
bill note [+] *f*; facture *f*; relevé *m*; quittance *f*
bind (to) lier *v*
bit (of tool) fer *m*
bitumen bitume *m*
blaze incendie *m*
bleed-tap (of radiator) purgeur *m*

blind store *m*
block bloc *m*
block of flats immeuble *m*
blockage obstruction *f*
blow (to) (a fuse) griller *v*
blueprint plan *m*
board/floorboard planche [+] *f*
boarding; boarded fence palissade *f*
bog marais *m*
boiler chaudière [+] *f*
bolt; door bolt verrou *m*
bond-stone parpaing *m*
book-keeper comptable *m/f*
book-keeping comptabilité *f*
border tile (wall tile) listel *m*
borrow (to) emprunter *v*
boundary fence clôture *f* de bornage
boundary marking bornage *m*
boundary stone or marker borne *f*
box room reduit *m*; débarras *m*
brace or strut (carpentry) contrevent *m*
brad pointe *f*
branch (of a bank) agence [+] *f*
branch-pipe branchement *m*
branching branchement *m*
brass laiton *m*
breadth largeur *f*
break (off) (to) (a contract) rompre *v*
breeze block aggloméré *m*; parpaing *m*
brick (to) maçonner *v*; murer *v*
brick or stone laying maçonnerie *f*
brick up (to) murer *v*; maçonner *v*
bricklayer maçon *m*
brickwork; stonework maçonnerie *f*
bridge pont *m*
brush/paintbrush brosse *f*
brushwood broussailles *fpl*; taillis *m*
bucket seau *m*
buckle (to) (metal) voiler *v*
build (to) bâtir *v*; construire *v*; édifier *v*
builder constructeur *m*; maçon *m*
building bâtiment [+] *m*; construction *f*; immeuble *m*; édifice *m*; *(colloq)* bâtisse *f*
building land/site terrain *m*
building permit permis *m* de construire
building rubble or debris décombres *mpl*
building site chantier *m* (de construction)
building work ouvrage *m*
building works travaux *mpl*
building, main corps *m* de bâtiment

built-up area agglomération *f*; zone *f* bâtie
bulb (electric light) ampoule *f*
bulb socket; lamp holder douille *f*
bull's eye window; round window
    œil-de-bœuf *m*
burden (to) grever *v*
burn out (to) (electric motor, light bulb)
    griller *v*
business contract (eg building work contract)
    contrat *m* d'entreprise
buy (to) acheter *v*; acquérir *v*
buyer acheteur *m*; acheteuse *f*; acquéreur *m*
buying acquisition *f*

C

cabin cabanon *m*; cabane *f*; chalet *m*
cabinet (furniture) cabinet *m*
cabinet-maker ébéniste *m/f*; menuisier *m* d'art
cable câble *m*
cable duct conduit *m*; caniveau *m*; canalisation *f*
cables (elect) canalisation *f*
cadastral register cadastre *m*
cadastral survey cadastre *m*
calculation compte ⁺ *m*
canalisation canalisation *f*
cancellation résiliation ⁺ *f*
capacity (content, area) contenance *f*
capital capital *m*
caretaker; keeper gardien *m*; gardienne *f*
carpenter (assembly of roof timbers, etc)
    charpentier *m*
carpenter (joiner) menuisier *m*
carpentry charpente *f* en bois
carpentry (joinery) menuiserie *f*
carpet, fitted moquette *f*
carry (to) porter *v*
carrying out (eg building work) mise *f* en
    œuvre
carve (to) (wood) tailler *v*
casing (of a machine) habillage *m*
cast iron fonte ⁺ *f*
casting fonte ⁺ *f*
castle château *m*
cattle-shed étable *f*
ceiling plafond ⁺ *m*
ceiling void vide *m* sous plafond
cellar cave *m*
cement ciment ⁺ *m*

cement block foundation blocage *m*
cement covering chape *f* ciment
cement rendering crépi *m*
cement/concrete mixer bétonnière *f*
certificate acte *m* (see also extrait); attestation *f*
certificate of conformity certificat *m* de
    conformité
certificate of local planning provisions
    certificat *m* d'urbanisme
certified copy of l'acte de vente expédition *f*
certified report constat *m*
chalet chalet *m*; bungalow *m*; cabanon *m*
change (to) transformer *v*
change of ownership mutation *f*
characteristic propriété *f*
charge servitude ⁺ *f*
charge (tax, levy) perception *f*
charge (commission) prélèvement *m*
charge(s) frais *m/mpl*
cheque chèque *m*
chimes sonnerie *f*
chimney (stack) cheminée *f*
chimney stack (above roof level) souche *f*
chimney sweep ramoneur *m*
chimney sweep's brush hérisson *m*
chipboard; particle board aggloméré *m*
chromium chrome *m*
circuit (elect) circuit *m*
circuit-breaker (trip switch) disjoncteur *m*
circuit-breaker; fuse; cut-out (elect)
    coupe-circuit *m*
circuit wiring câblage *m* de circuit
cistern citerne *f*; cuve *f*
civil engineering génie civil *m*
cladding revêtement *m*; lambris *m*
claim droit ⁺ *m*
clamping; locking blocage *m*
clarification mise *f* au point
clause clause ⁺ *f*
clean net, nette *adj*
clean (to) nettoyer *v*
clean down (brickwork, etc) (to) ragréer *v*
cleaning nettoiement *m*; nettoyage *m*
cleaning/sweeping a chimney or flue
    ramonage *m*
cleanse (to) nettoyer *v*
cleansing assainissement *m*
clear (to) vider *v*; nettoyer *v*
clearance; riddance débarras *m*
clearing (of ground, wood etc) défrichage *m*;

défrichement *m*
closed clos,-e *adj*
closet cabinet *m*
cluster of buildings corps *m* de bâtiment
co-ownership; joint ownership copropriété *f*
coat enduit *m*
coat (of paint, etc) couche *f*
coat of rough-cast or plaster ravalement *m*
coating enduit *m*; revêtement *m*
coating of fill-in material (eg plaster) solin *m*
cob; wattle and daub torchis *m*
cobbled road chaussée *f* pavée
collateral garantie *f*; nantissement *m*
collection (tax, charge) perception *f*
collector collecteur *m*
colour couleur *f*; coloris *m*
colour wash badigeon *m*
commitment engagement *m*
common ownership (eg of a wall or fence)
  mitoyenneté *f*
common parts of property parties *fpl*
  communes
commune commune *f*
community communauté *f*
compilation (of inventory) confection *f*
complete (to) achever *v*
completion achèvement *m*
component élément [+] *m*
comprehensive household insurance assurance
  f multirisque(s) habitation
concrete béton *m*
concrete block (with air channels) parpaing *m*
concrete wall voile *f*
condensation condensation *f*
condition condition [+] *f*; préalable *m*
conduct conduite *f*
conduit conduite *f*; conduit *m*; tuyau *m*
conduit (wiring/cable) canalisation *f*
conflagration incendie *m*
connect (to) (electrically) monter *v*
connecting raccordement *m*
connection branchement *m*
conservatory (attached to house) serre *f*
consider (to) projeter *v*
consignment expédition *f*
consignment (of merchandise) consignation *f*
constraint astreinte *f*
constraints servitudes *fpl*
construct (to) bâtir *v*; construire *v*; édifier *v*
construction construction *f*

construction contract contrat *m* de construction
construction fault/defect vice *m* de construction
construction permissible constructible *adj*
constructor constructeur *m*
consumer (gas, electricity etc) abonné *m*;
  abonnée *f*
consumption (of electricity) consommation *f* de
  courant; dépense *f*
contract contrat *m*; forfait *m*; entreprise *f*
contract of sale of a dwelling for construction
  contrat *m* de vente d'immeuble à construire
contract price; all-inclusive price prix *m*
  forfaitaire
contractor entrepreneur *m*
contribution cotisation *f*; apport *m*;
  prestation *f*; quote-part *f*
control réglementation *f*
conurbation agglomération *f*
conversion aménagement *m*
convert (to) aménager [+] *v*; convertir *v*
converting aménagement *m*
cooker cuisinière [+] *f*
copper cuivre *m*
coppice taillis *m*
copse taillis *m*; bosquet *m*
copy exemplaire *m*; transcription *f*
cord (of electric appliance) fil [+] *m*
cork liège *m*
cork (stopper) bouchon *m*
corner coin *m*
corner kitchen coin-cuisine *m*
cost coût *m*; frais [+] *m/mpl*; valeur *f*
cottage chaumière *f*; maison *f* de campagne;
  mazet *m*; villa *f*
cottage, lightly-built pavillon *m*
council offices mairie *f*
count compte [+] *m*; décompte *m*
counter compteur [+] *m*
counterfoil talon *m*
country house manoir *m*
country house (S. France) bastide *f*
countryside; open country campagne *f*
court/courtyard cour *f*
cover abri *m*; enveloppe *f*
cover (to) tapisser *v*
cover a roof with zinc (to) zinguer *v*
covered porch with an outside staircase
  perron *m*
covering revêtement *m*
cowshed étable *f*

crack lézarde *f*; fêlure *f*
crack (to) fêler (se) *v*
craftsman artisan *m*
credit crédit *m*
credit transfer virement *m*
creditor créancier *m*; créancière *f*
crevice; split (eg in wall) lézarde *f*
crude brut,-e *adj*
crumbling; dilapidated (eg wall) délabré *adj*
cubbyhole reduit *m*
cupboard placard *m*; armoire *f*
current courant *m*
current consumption (elect) consommation *f* de courant
cut coupure *f*
cut (to) couper *v*
cut (to) (stone) tailler *v*
cut off (to) couper *v*
cutting coupure *f*
cutting edge (of a tool) fil ‡ *m*
cutting back (agric) ravalement *m*

D

daily fine for contract delay astreinte *f*
damage dégât ‡ *m*; dommage *m*
damp-proof course couche *f* d'étanchéité
date of maturity; due date échéance *f*
deadline délai *m*; échéance *f*
death duties droits *mpl* de succession
debiting prélèvement *m*
decorative cladding habillage *m*
decorator décorateur *m*; décoratrice *f*
deduction déduction *f*; abattement *m*; décompte *m*; prélèvement *m*
deed acte ‡ *m*; contrat *m*
deed executed by a notaire acte *m* authentique
deed of conveyance acte *m* authentique; acte *m* de vente
default défaut ‡ *m*
defect défaut *m*; vice ‡ *m*
defect (due to bad workmanship) malfaçon *f*
definitive définitif,-ive *adj*
delay délai *m*
deliver (to) remettre *v*; livrer *v*
delivery livraison *f*; remise *f*
demolish (to) démolir *v*
department (French administrative region) département *m*

dependence dépendance *f*
deposit acompte *m*; arrhes *fpl*; consignation *f*; dépôt ‡ *m*
deposit (to) (money) déposer *v*; verser *v*
deposit of guarantee caution *f*
depositary séquestre *m*
depot dépôt *m*
depth profondeur *f*; épaisseur *f*
descriptive signalétique *adj*
design dessin *m*
designer dessinateur *m*; dessinatrice *f*
designer (interior) architecte *m* d'intérieur; ensemblier *m*
desk bureau *m*
detailed account décompte *m*
details renseignement *m*
determination clause (for a contract) clause *f* résolutoire
develop (to) aménager ‡ *v*
developer maître *m* d'ouvrage *m*; promoteur *m*
developing mise *f* au point
development (housing) lotissement *m*
development (improvement) aménagement *m*
development (of project) déroulement *m*
diagram schéma *m*; schème *m*
digging fouille *f*
dilapidated (eg house) délabré *adj*
disaster sinistre ‡ *m*
discharge décharge *f*
discount abattement *m*; décompte *m*; remise *f*
discuss (to) (a problem) discuter *v*
dishwasher lave-vaisselle *m*
dismissal radiation *f*
disorder désordre *m*
dispatch expédition *f*
displace (to) déplacer *v*
disposal disposition *f*
distemper badigeon *m*
distemper (to) badigeonner *v*
distraint saisie *f*
distribution répartition *f*
distribution box coffret *m* de distribution; coffret de répartition
distribution network réseau *m* de distribution
district quartier *m*; commune *f*
ditch fossé *m*
divide (up) (to) partager *v*
divided into plots parcellaire *adj*
dividing up (into lots) lotissement *m*
division partage *m*

division (room) cloison *f*
DIY (to) bricoler *v*
DIY, do-it-yourself (materials) bricolage *m*
do odd jobs (to) bricoler *v*
do repairs (to) bricoler *v*
do-it-yourself (job, activity) bricolage *m*
docket bordereau *m*
document document *m*
documentation dossier *m*
domain domaine *m*
domestic electrical appliances électroménager *m*
door porte [+] *f*
door post jambage *m*
door sill seuil *m*
doorstep pas *m* de porte; seuil *m*
doorway embrasure *f* de porte
dormer window lucarne *f*
dossier dossier *m*
double glazing double vitrage *m*
doubling doublage *m*
dovecot colombier *m*; pigeonnier *m*
draft (eg of a contract) projet *m*
draft (to) (a document) rédiger *v*
draft project/draft scheme avant-projet *m*
drafting (of a document) rédaction *f*
drain égout *m*
drain (bottom outlet) bouche *f* d'égout
drain (to) vider *v*
drain off (to) (water, oil) vidanger *v*
drain-cock purgeur *m*
drainage (land) drainage *m*; assèchement *m*
drainage (run-off) écoulement *m*
draining well puisard *m*
draining assèchement *m*
draughtsman dessinateur *m*
draughtswoman dessinatrice *f*
draw up (to) (a contract) rédiger *v*
draw up (to) (eg plans) établir *v*
drawing dessin *m*; plan [+] *m*
drawing paper papier *m* à dessin
drawing up (a contract) passation *f*; rédaction *f*
drawing up (of deed, will) confection *f*
drenching douche *f*
dresser vaisselier *m*
drier séchoir [+] *m*
drip proof imperméable *adj*
drop chute *f*
drying out assèchement *m*
drying room séchoir *m*
duct; ducting conduite *f*

due droit [+] *m*
dues cotisation *f*; redevance *f*
dump (to) (rubbish) déposer *v*
dust poussière *f*
dustbin/rubbish bin poubelle *f*; boîte *f* à ordures
duty taxe *f*
dwelling demeure *f*; habitation [+] *f*; logis *m*
dwelling house logement *m*

E

earth terre [+] *f*; sol [+] *m*
earth (elect) terre [+] *f*; masse *f*
earthenware (glazed) faïence *f*
earthenware factory faïencerie *f*
earthwork(s) terrassement *m*
ease aisance *f*
easement servitude *f*
eaves égout *m*; égout *m* du bord du toit; avant-toit *m*
edge rebord *m*
edge-plate (of lock) rebord *m*
edifice édifice *m*
elect (to) élire *v*
electrical fittings équipement *m* électrique
electrician électricien *m*
electricity électricité *f*
electricity supply alimentation *f* en électricité
element élément *m*
elevation hauteur *f*
elevator ascenseur *m*
eligible party ayant droit *m*; ayants droit pl; ayant cause *m*
embankment terrassement *m*
embed (to) sceller *v*
empty vide *adj*
empty (to) vider *v*; vidanger *v*
empty space vide *m*
enclosed clos,-e *adj*
enclosure clôture [+] *f*
encumber (to) grever *v*
encumbrance servitude *f*
end (to) (eg building work) achever *v*
endorsement avenant *m*
engineer ingénieur *m*
enjoyment jouissance *f*
entail (to) (an estate) grever *v*
enterprise entreprise *f*

entrance entrée *f*
entry (into accounts ledger) passation *f*
equip (to) équiper *v*; aménager ‡ *v*
equipment matériel *m*; matériels *pl*; outillage *m*
erect (to) bâtir *v*; édifier *v*
establish (to) établir *v*
estate avoir *m*; bien *m*; domaine *m*; fonds *m*;
   patrimoine *m*; propriété *f*
estate agent agent *m* immobilier
estate duties droits *mpl* de succession
estimate devis ‡ *m*
estimate of quantities and costs mètré *m*
eviction; dispossession éviction *f*
examine (to) (a question) discuter *v*; examiner *v*
excavation terrassement *m*; excavation *f*;
   fouille *f*
excavation site fouille *f*
excavation work terrasse *f*
exclusive of tax/excluding taxes hors taxe *adj*;
   HT *abb*
exemption (from tax) dégrèvement *m*
expenses/expenditure frais ‡ *m/mpl*;
   dépense *f*
expert expert *m*
expert valuation/appraisal expertise *f*
expiry date échéance *f*
expose (to) exposer *v*
exposition énoncé *m*
express (to) énoncer *v*
extension of payment period prorogation ‡ *f*
extension agrandissement *m*
extension of time prorogation ‡ *f*
exterior extérieur *m*; (also *adj*)
exterior fittings équipement *m* extérieur
extract extrait *m*

F

fabricate (to) fabriquer *v*
facade façade *f*
face parement *m*
face (to) maçonner *v*
facilities/amenities les équipements *mpl*
facility aisance *f*
facing revêtement *m*; parement *m*
facing south/north/east/west exposé au sud/
   nord/est/ouest
fall chute *f*
fall due (to) venir *v* à échéance

falling due/payable échéant *adj*
false ceiling faux-plafond *m*
family mansion maison *f* de maître
fan ventilateur *m*
fanlight imposte *f*
farm ferme *f*
farm building(s) corps *m* de ferme
farm rent fermage *m*
farmhouse ferme *f*; maison *f* de ferme
farmhouse, small fermette *f*
farmyard cour *f* de ferme
fasten (to) lier *v*
fault défaut *m*; désordre *m*; malfaçon *f*; vice *m*
fault, latent or hidden vice *m* caché
fee redevance *f*; cotisation *f*
fee(s) honoraires *mpl*; frais *m/mpl*
felt/felting feutre *m*
felting feutrage *m*
fence; fencing clôture *f*; palissade *f*
field champ *m*
field (enclosed) clos *m*
filament (of electric bulb) fil ‡ *m*
file dossier *m*
filler mastic *m*
fillet-gutter solin *m*
final définitif,ive *adj*
final conveyance document acte *m* de vente;
   acte *m* authentique de vente; acte *m* définitif
finalising/settling (business) mise *f* au point
finish (to) achever *v*
finished achevé,-e *adj*
finishing finition ‡ *f*
fire (accidental) incendie *m*
fire hydrant bouche *f* d'incendie
fire insurance assurance *f* incendie
fireplace cheminée *f*
firm; company entreprise *f*
fishpond réservoir *m*
fit (to) poser *v*; équiper *v*
fit out (to) aménager *v*; installer *v*
fitter installateur *m*
fitting out équipement *m*; aménagement *m*
fittings/fitments équipement *m*
fix (to) (a price) établir *v*
fixed price or rate forfait *m*
flag; flagstone dalle *f*
flagging/flagstones dallage *m*
flagging laid on foundation of large stones
   hérisson *m*
flap trappe *f*

flashing between wall and abutting roof
solin *m*
flat appartement *m*; logement *m*
flat (ground floor) rez-de-chaussée *m*; rdc
(*abb*)
flat roof terrasse *f*
flaw vice [+] *m*
flex, heavy-duty câble *m*
floor sol *m*
floor, first/second premier/deuxième étage *m*
floor/flooring plancher *m*
floor level étage *m*; niveau *m*
floorboard planche *f*
flow; outflow écoulement *m*
flue carneau *m*; tuyau *m*; conduit *m* de
cheminée
flue brush hérisson *m*
flue, boiler carneau *m* de chaudière
flushing cistern of WC chasse *f* d'eau
food; groceries alimentation *f*
footing semelle *f*
for life viager *adj*
forbidden; prohibited; banned interdit,-e *adj*
foreclosure saisie *f*
foreman/forewoman contremaître *m*;
contremaîtresse *f*
forest forêt *f*
forfeit deposit dédit *m*
form modalité *f*
formal deed (of sale) acte *m* authentique;
acte *m* (authentique) de vente
formal demand/notice mise *f* en demeure
former ancien, ancienne *adj*
foundation fondation *f*; fondement *m*
**foundation consisting of a next-to-earth
compacted layer of large stones** hérisson *m*
foundation wall jambage *m*
foundations and walls gros œuvre *m*
frame (door or window) châssis *m*; huisserie *f*
frame(work) (of house, building) charpente *f*
framework ossature *f*
framework of beams poutrage *m*; poutraison *f*
free of (eg tax) net, nette *adj*
French Land Commission S.A.F.E.R. *f*;
(Société d'Aménagement Foncier et
d'Établissement Rural)
French Standards Association AFNOR;
Association Française de Normalisation
front façade *f*
front entrance (archit) portail *m*

front steps (of a house) perron *m*
fuel briquette aggloméré *m*
fund(s) fonds *m*; capital *m*
furnace four *m*
furnish (to) meubler [+] *v*
furniture; furnishing ameublement *m*;
mobilier *m*
furniture, well-made meubles *mpl* de bonne
facture
fuse fusible *m*
fuse box boîte *f* à fusibles; porte-fusibles *m*

G

gable pignon *m*
gain in value plus-value *f*
galvanize (to) galvaniser *v*
gamut gamme *f*
gang équipe *f*
gap vide *m*
garage garage *m*
garbage ordures [+] *fpl*
garden jardin *m*
garrigue garrigue *f*
gas gaz *m*
gas fitter gazier *m*
gas supply alimentation *f* en gaz
gasket joint *m*
gate porte [+] *f*; portail *m*
gate (metal) grille *f*; portail *m* métallique
gate; double gates portail *m*
geologist géologue *m/f*
geometrician/geometer géomètre *m*
girder solive *f*; poutre *f*; ferme *f*
girderage poutrage *m*; poutraison *f*
give precise details (to) préciser *v*
give up (to) renoncer *v*
glass door vitrage *m*
glass items vitrerie *f*
glass partition vitrage *m*
glass-wool laine *f* de verre
glasshouse serre *f*
glaze (to) vitrer *v*
glazier vitrier *m*
glaziery vitrerie *f*
glazing vitrage *m*; vitrerie *f*
goods biens *mpl*
gradient pente *f*
grain (of wood) fil [+] *m*

granite granit *m*
grass gazon *m*; herbe *f*
grassland prairie *f*
grating grille *f*
gravel gravier *m*
gravel (to) (eg roadway) empierrer *v*
grazing pacage *m*
grazing land pacage *m*
greenhouse serre f
grid (electricity) réseau *m*; grille *f*
grille grille *f*
gross (eg weight, cost) brut,-e *adj*
ground terrain *m*; terre *f*; sol *m*
ground floor rez-de-chaussée (rdc) *m*; sol *m*
grounds (of a mansion or chateau) parc *m*
grout (to) jointoyer *v*
grout in (to) sceller *v*
grove bosquet *m*
guarantee garantie *f*; caution *f*
guardian curateur *m*; curatrice *f*
guardianship curatelle *f*; tutelle *f*
gutter (road) caniveau *m*
gutter (roof) gouttière *f*; chéneau *m*

H

habitation tax taxe *f* d'habitation
haggle (to) (over a price) discuter *v*
half-timbering colombage *m*
hall entrée *f*; vestibule *m*
hall (of a chateau) salle *f*
hallway entrée *f*
hammer marteau *m*
handyman; do-it-yourselfer bricoleur *m*
handywoman; do-it-yourselfer bricoleuse *f*
hardware quincaillerie *f*
harm dommage *m*
harm (to) nuire *v*
hatch trappe *f*
head office siège *m*
headquarters (of company) siège *m*
heating chauffage *m*
heating engineer chauffagiste *m*
hectare (10,000 sq. metres = 2.4711 acres) hectare *m*; ha (*abb*)
hedge haie *f*; clôture *f*
heel talon *m*
height (person) taille *f*
height hauteur *f*

high or thick wall muraille *f*
highway system voirie *f*
hinge; butt-hinge charnière *f*
hinge (cabinet); hinge pin fiche *f*
hold prise *f*
hole trou $^+$ *m*
hole for rainwater pipe souillarde *f*
home logis *m*
hose tuyau *m*
hot water tank ballon *m* d'eau chaude
hot water tank with immersion heater cumulus *m* électrique
house maison $^+$ *f*; logement *m*; habitation $^+$ *f*; pavillon $^+$ *m*
house associated with a vineyard château *m*
house in isolated area chartreuse *f*
house in the countryside maison *f* de campagne
house joined each side maisons *fpl* mitoyennes
house, country or town, architecturally superior maison *f* de maître
house, three-storeyed house maison *f* à deux étages
house, long, small (Brittany); fisherman's house panty *m*
house(s), semi-detached maison *f* jumelle; maisons *fpl* mitoyennes
housing development ensemble *m*; lotissement *m*
housing estate or site lotissement *m*
hunt for (to) rechercher *v*
hut; cabin loge *f*; cabanon *m*; mazet *m*

IJK

identifying signalétique *adj*
illumination éclairage *m*
immersion heater thermoplongeur *m*
immobilization (of capital, etc) immobilisation *f*
impermeable imperméable *adj*
imperviousness étanchéité *f*
implementation (eg of a regulation) mise *f* en œuvre
implements outillage *m*
imposing house with land demeure *f*
in addition en plus
in good condition (of a property) bon êtat *m*
inclusive of tax; all taxes included TTC; T.T.C.; toutes taxes *fpl* comprises

income revenu *m*; rente *f*
increase in value plus-value *f*
index card fiche *f*
information renseignement *m*
inheritance tax droits *mpl* de succession
injury dommage *m*
inlet/intake prise *f*
inn auberge *f*; logis *m*
inside intérieur *m*; also *adj*
inspection hole/window regard *m*
install (to) installer *v*; poser *v*
install fitments (to) équiper *v*
installation installation *f*; branchement *m*
installing installation *f*
instalment acompte‡*m*; versement ‡ *m*
insulation isolation ‡ *f*; isolement *m*
insulator isolateur *m*
insurance assurance *f*
insurance against building faults assurance *f*
    dommage(s)-ouvrage; dommages-ouvrage *m*
insurance premium prime *f* d'assurance
intended use of a building destination *f* d'une
    bâtiment
interest intérêt *m*
interior intérieur *m*; also *adj*
interior surface paroi *f*
intermediate ceiling faux-plafond *m*
inventory of fixtures état *m* des lieux
invoice facture *f*; note *f*
invoice (to) facturer *v*
iron fer *m*
iron or steel sheet tôle *f*
ironmonger's (shop) quincaillerie *f*
ironmonger/hardware dealer quincaillier m,
    quincaillière *f*
ironmongery quincaillerie *f*
isolation isolement *m*
item in contract clause *f*; prescription *f*;
    stipulation *f*
jacket (lagging) enveloppe *f*
jamb/jamb-post jambage *m*
join together (to) assembler *v*
join together (to) (eg with tie or strap) lier *v*
joiner menuisier *m*
joinery menuiserie *f*
joining raccordement *m*
joint (to) (carpentry) assembler *v*
joint joint *m*
joint possession; joint ownership indivision *f*
joist solive *f*

joisting solivage *m*
junction branchement *m*
junction box (elect); connecting box (elect)
    boîte *f* de derivation; boîte *f* de jonction
key clé ou clef\ *f*
kitchen cuisine *f*
kitchen garden potager *m*
kitchen cooker/range cuisinière ‡ *f*
kitchenette coin-cuisine *m*; kitchenette *f*

L

labour main-d'œuvre *f*
labour force main-d'œuvre *f*
ladder échelle *f*
lagging (heat insulation) habillage *m*;
    enveloppe *f*
lake lac *m*
lamp luminaire *m*
land terrain *m*; terre ‡ *f*; fonds *m*
Land Charges Registry bureau *m* de
    conservation des hypothèques
land register/registry cadastre *m*
land surveying arpentage *m*
land tax taxe *f* foncière
landing (of a staircase) palier *m*
landscape paysage *m*
lane chemin *m*; voie *f*
lattice treillis *m*; treillage *m*; claire-voie *f*;
    claires-voies *pl*
laundry room buanderie *f*
law droit *m*
lawn pelouse *f*; gazon *m*
lawyer avocat *m*; avocate *f*; conseiller *m*
    juridique; conseillère *f* juridique
lay (to) poser *v*
lay bricks (to) maçonner *v*; murer *v*
lay bricks or stone (to) maçonner *v*
lay down (to) déposer *v*
lay out (to) aménager *v*
lay-out disposition *f*
layer couche *f*
laying/layer of stones forming bedding for
    flagstones or solid flooring hérissonnage *m*
laying double doublage *m*
laying out (of ground plan) implantation *f*
lead (metal) plomb *m*
leadwork plomberie *f*
lean-to appentis *m*; hangar *m*

lease bail *m*; location-bail *f*
leaseback cession-bail *f*
leasehold location-bail *f*; fermage *m*
leasing location-bail *f*; crédit-bail *m*
ledge saillie *f*
legal adviser conseiller *m* juridique; conseillère *f* juridique
legal document acte [+] *m*
legal flaw or irregularity vice *m* de forme
legal representative of person or company syndic *m*
legal successor ayant droit *m*; ayants droit pl; ayant cause *m*
lend (to) prêter *v*
length longueur *f*
lessee locataire *f*
letting location *f*
level niveau *m*
levy prélèvement *m*; perception *f*
licence fee (eg television) redevance *f*
life annuity viager *m*; also *adj*
lift ascenseur *m*
light lumière *f*
light (lamp) luminaire *m*
light (to) (a fire, cigar etc) allumer *v*
lighting (elect) éclairage *m*
lighting (fire) allumage *m*
limit borne *f*
line (to) tapisser *v*
linen room lingerie *f*
lining revêtement *m* enduit; doublage *m*; lambris *m*
lining (eg of a well, cellar) cuvelage *m*; cuvellement *m*
list liste *f*
litigant plaideur *m*; plaideuse *f*; partie *f*
living room séjour *m*; salon *m*
load-shedding (of electricity) délestage *m*
loan prêt [+] *m*; emprunt *m*
local local, -e *adj*
local electricity supply area secteur *m*
locality; named place lieudit, lieu-dit *m*
locating implantation *f*
lock serrure *f*
lodge loge *f*; pavillon [+] *m*; maisonnette *f*
lodge (to) (a document) déposer *v*
lodging logement *m*
loft grenier *m*
loggia loge *f*
lone cottage or lodge chartreuse *f*

long barn or house; Breton farmhouse longère *f*
look for (to) rechercher *v*
loss dommage *m*
lounge salon *m*; séjour *m*
lounge suite (furniture) salon *m*
louvred or slatted shutters (S. France) persiennes *fpl*
lower ground floor (of shop) sous-sol *m*
lumber room débarras *m*
lump sum prix *m* à forfait; somme *f* forfaiture
lump-sum contract forfait [+] *m*

M

machinery machines *fpl*
mahogany acajou *m*
main building corps *m* de bâtiment
main drain/sewer collecteur [+] *m* à l'égout; collecteur [+] *m* principal
main home domicile *m* principal
mains drainage tout-à-l'égout *m*
maintain (to) entretenir *v*
maintenance entretien *m*
maisonette maisonnette *f*; duplex *m*
make facture *f*
make (to) fabriquer *v*
make clear (to) préciser *v*
make fast (to) assujettir *v*
make out (to) (a cheque) rédiger *v*
make use of mise *f* en œuvre
making confection *f*
man-hole regard *m*; trou *m* d'homme; bouche *f* d'égout
management gestion *f*; direction *f*
manager; managing agent gérant *m*; gérante *f*
mandatary mandataire *m*
mandate mandat *m*
manor house manoir *m*; chartreuse *f*
manor house (small) gentilhommière *f*
manpower main-d'œuvre *f*
mansard (roof) mansarde *f*
mansion, country château *m*
mansion, family maison *f* de maître
mantlepiece cheminée *f*
manufacture facture [+] *f*
manufacture (to) fabriquer *v*
marble marbre *m*
market marché *m*

45

marsh/marshland marais *m*
mas mas *m*
mason maçon *m*
masonry maçonnerie *f*
masonry paint (textured) crépi *m*
masonry; bricks and mortar bâtisse *f*
mass masse *f*
massive structure masse *f*
master key passe-partout *m*
mastic mastic *m*
material; materials matériau *m*;
    matériaux *mpl*
mayor; mayoress (seldom used) maire *m*;
    mairesse *f*
meadow pré *m*; prairie *f*
means modalité *f*
measurement métrage *m*; mètré *m*
measuring area of land in ares aréage *m*
mechanically controlled ventilation ventilation
    f mécanique controlée; V.M.C.; VMC *abb*
Mediterranean style house mas *m*
melting fonte *f*
mend (to) réparer *v*
mending réparation *f*
metal (to) empierrer *v*
metal grilles etc métallerie *f*
metalwork métallerie *f*
metal, metals métal m, métaux *mpl*
meter compteur ⁺ *m*
meter reading relevé *m* du compteur
method modalité *f*
metre; metre rule mètre *m*
metric length métrage *m*
mezzanine/mezzanine floor mezzanine étage *m*
mildew moisissure *f*
mill moulin ⁺ *m*
mineral wool/rock wool laine *f* minérale; laine *f*
    de roche
minutes procès-verbal *m*; procès-verbaux *mpl*;
mirror industry/trade miroiterie *f*
modality modalité *f*
mode modalité *f*
modern architecture architecture *f* moderne
modern house villa *f*
modernisation modernisation *f*; rénovation *f*
modernise (to) moderniser *v*; rénover *v*
modify (to) modifier *v*
mortar mortier *m*
mortar in (to) sceller *v*
mortgage hypothèque *f*

Mortgage Registry; Land Charges Registry
    bureau *m* de conservation des hypothèques
mould moisissure *f*
moulding moulure *f*
mount (to) monter *v*
movable meuble *adj*
move (to) déplacer *v*
moving (house) déménagement *m*
mutual benefit insurance company mutuelle *f*

N

nail clou *m*; pointe *f*
nail (to)/nail down (to) clouer *v*
National Federation of Estate Agents (France)
    FNAIM, Fédération Nationale des Agents
    Immobiliers et Mandataires en vente de Fonds
negotiate (to) négocier *v*
negotiation négociation *f*
negotiator interlocuteur *m*; interlocutrice *f*
neighbourhood voisinage *m*; quartier *m*
net (eg price, weight, etc) net, nette *adj*
network réseau ⁺ *m*
new neuf, neuve *adj*
noise bruit ⁺ *m*
noise level niveau *m* de bruit
noise reduction réduction *f* de bruit
nook reduit *m*; recoin *m*
not in accordance with non-conformité *f*
notary notaire *m*
note (delivery, credit, etc) bordereau *m*
note (written) note *f*
**notification that permitted building work is
    completed** déclaration *f* d'achèvement des
    travaux

O

oak chêne *m*
obstruction obstruction *f*
offer offre *f*; offre *f* de prix
office bureau *m*; cabinet ⁺ *m*
office of mayor mairie *f*
Office of Mortgages and Land Registry
    bureau *m* des hypothèques
old ancien, ancienne *adj*
one hundred square metres are *m*
one-room flat studio *m*; studette *f*
open-work (fence, gate, etc) claire-voie *f*;

claires-voies *pl*
opening (window, door) baie *f*
opening orifice *m*
orchard verger *m*; clos *m*
order arrêté *m*; ordre *m*
orifice orifice *m*
origin origine $^+$ *f*
outbuilding dépendance *f*
outer walls gros œuvre *m*
outhouse hangar *m*
outlet décharge *f*
outline (of a project) esquisse *f*
outside extérieur *m*; also *adj*
oven four *m*
overdue arriéré,-e *adj*
overdue/owing en arriéré
overestimate/overvalue (to) surestimer *v*
overflow (pipe) trop-plein *m*
owner (commissioning building work)
    maître *m* d'ouvrage
owner propriétaire *m*
ownership propriété *f*

P

pail seau *m*
pailful/bucketful seau *m*
paint peinture $^+$ *f*
paint (to) peindre *v*
paintbrush brosse *f*; pinceau *m*
painter peintre *m/f*
painting peinture $^+$ *f*
paintwork peinture $^+$ *f*
pair of steps escabeau *m*
paling clôture $^+$ *f*
pane (window glass) vitre *f*; carreau *m*
panel panneau $^+$ *m*
panel (to) lambrisser *v*
panelling boiserie *f*; lambris *m*; lambrissage *m*
parcel (of land) parcelle *f*
park parc *m*
parquet or wooden floor parquet *m*
part partie *f*
particular(s) renseignement *m*
partition/partition wall cloison $^+$ *f*; cloison
    mitoyenne; paroi *f*
party partie *f*
passage passage $^+$ *m*
passage (in apartment) dégagement *m*

pasture land pacage *m*
pasturing pacage *m*
path chemin *m*
pave (to) daller *v*
pavilion pavillon $^+$ *m*
paving stone dalle *f*
paving/pavement dallage *m*
pay (to) verser *v*
pay a bill (to) régler *v* une facture
payment paiement *m*; versement *m*; règlement *m*
payment on account acompte *m*
payment, overdue paiement *m* arriéré
pedestal socle *m*
pedestal (of washbasin) colonne *f*
peephole regard *m*
penalty dédit *m*; astreinte *f*
pension rente *f*
penthouse auvent *m*; étage *m* hors-toit
penthouse roof appentis *m*
percentage (of) pourcentage *m* (de)
perfecting mise *f* au point
**period house (eg built early part of 20th
    century)** maison *f* bourgeoise
permanent définitif,-ive *adj*
permit to demolish a building permis *m* de
    démolir
perpend parpaing *m*
person interlocuteur *m*; interlocutrice *f*
person/private individual particulier *m*
person signing a contract partie *f*
phase/live wire (elect) phase *f*
picket piquet *m*
piece of furniture meuble *m*
piece of joinery/carpentry menuiserie *f*
piece of land terrain *m*
piece of work œuvre *f*
pied-à-terre pied-à-terre *m*
pig iron fonte $^+$ *f*
pigeon house/loft pigeonnier *m*; colombier *m*
pigsty porcherie *f*; étable *f* à porceaux
pile (constr) pieu *m*; pilotis *m*
pilot study avant-projet *m*
pipe tuyau $^+$ *m*; conduit *m*; tube *m*; conduite *f*
pipe fitter tuyauteur *m*; poseur *m/f* de tuyaux
pipes tuyauterie *f*; canalisation *f*
pipework canalisation *f*
pipework installation tuyauterie *f*
piping tuyauterie *f*
pit fosse *f*
pitch bitume *m*

pitch (slope) pente *f*; chute *f*
placing (an order) passation *f*
placing (eg of concrete) mise *f* en œuvre
plan plan *m*; projet *m*; schéma *m*; schème *m*
plan (to) projeter *v*
plan of land occupancy (official plan) Plan *m* d'Occupation des Sols; POS
plane plan *m*
plank planche *f*
planning permission permis *m* de construire
plant (equipment) matériel *m*; matériels *mpl*; also *adj*
plaster plâtre *m*
plaster (to) plâtrer *v*
plaster over (to)/render (to) plâtrer *v*
plaster rendering enduit *m*
plasterer plâtrier *m*
plate plaque *f*; tôle *f*
pledge nantissement *m*
plinth plinthe *f*; socle *m*
plot (of land) terrain *m*; parcelle *f* de terre; lotissement *m*
plug bouchon *m*
plug (elect) fiche *f*
plugging-in branchement *m*
plumb plomb *m*
plumb-bob plomb *m*
plumber plombier *m*
plumber's workshop plomberie *f*
plumbing plomberie *f*; robinetterie; installation *f* sanitaire
plumbline plomb *m*
point point *m*
point (elect) prise *f*
point (to) (masonry) jointoyer *v*
pointing (masonry) joint *m*
pole poteau *m*
policy (insurance) police *f*
porch/porchway porche *m*
portal portail *m*
possession bien *m*
possession of jouissance *f*
post poteau [+] *m*; piquet *m*; montant *m*
postpone (to) remettre *v*
postponement remise *f*
power pouvoir *m*
power (elect) courant *m*
power cut coupure *f*; délestage *m*
power of attorney procuration *f*; mandat *m*
power supply alimentation *f* en énergie

practicability viabilité *f*
pre-emptive right droits *mpl* de préemption
prejudice (to) nuire *v*
preliminary préalable *m*; also *adj*
preliminary agreement avant-contrat *m*
preliminary contract to sell promesse *f* de vente
preliminary version avant-projet *m*
premises local *m*; locaux *mpl*; lieux *mpl*; immeuble *m*
premises (business) locaux *mpl* commerciaux
preparation confection *f*
prescription prescription *f*
previous préalable *adj*
price prix *m*; montant *m*; valeur *f*
prime (to) (a pump) amorcer *v*
principal (in a transaction) mandant *m*; mandante *f*
principal residence domicile *m* principal
prior préalable *adj*
prior notice préavis *m*
private agreement by a document not legally certified acte *m* sous seing privé
private sale vente *f* à l'amiable
private/public law or right droit *m* privé/ public
probate duty droits *mpl* de succession
procedure démarche *f*; procédure *f*
professional expert *m*
professional association ordre *f*
progress déroulement *m*
progress report (eg of building work) compte-rendu *m*
project projet *m*; plan *m*
project (to) projeter *v*
project manager maître *m* d'œuvre
property propriété *f*; avoir *m*; bien *m*; domaine *m*
property developer promoteur *m* immobilier
property tax taxe *f* foncière
property transfer registration costs droits *mpl* d'enregistrement
proportion quotité *f*; taux *m*
proportional share quote-part *f*
proposed plan avant-projet *m*
protection abri *m*
provision prestation *f*; clause [‡] *f*; disposition *f*
provision (supply) apport *m*
proximity voisinage *m*
proxy procuration *f*; mandataire *m*; mandat *m*

pull down (to) démolir *v*
pumicing ponçage *m*
pump pompe ⁺ *f*
purchase acquisition *f*
purchase (to) acheter *v*
purchaser acheteur *m*; acheteuse *f*; acquéreur *m*
purlin panne *f*
put in (to) installer *v*; poser *v*
putting; setting mise *f*
putty mastic *m*
putty knife couteau *m* à mastiquer

Q

quantity surveying mètré *m*; métrage *m*
quantity surveyor métreur *m*; métreuse *f*
quarry stone moellon *m*
quarter quartier *m*
quit (to) or vacate (to) (premises) vider *v*
quota quotité *f*; quote-part *f*
quotation offre *m* de prix; devis *m*

R

rafter chevron *m*
raftering chevronnage *m*
rafters (roof) chevronnage *m*
railings grille *f*
railing, surrounding grille *f* de clôture
rain-water tank citerne *f*
range gamme *f*
rate taux *m*
ratio taux *m*
read, approved and agreed (endorsement put on a legal document, with signature) lu et approuvé, bon pour accord
reading (of meter) relevé *m*
real estate biens *mpl* immeubles; bien *m* fonds; immeuble *m*; propriété *f* foncière
rear arrière *m*
rebuilding reconstruction *f*
receipt reçu *m*; quittance *f*; réception *f*
receiver séquestre *m*
receiver (tank) collecteur *m*
reception réception *f*

recess recoin *m*
record fiche *f*
redecorate (to); repaint (to); redo (to) refaire *v*
redemption (eg of mortgage) dégagement ⁺ *m*
redevelopment réaménagement *m*; rénovation *f*
redressing (stonework) ravalement *m*
refrigerator réfrigérateur *m*
refurbish (to) remettre *v* à neuf; remettre *v* en état
refuse ordures *fpl*; détritus *mpl*
refuse collection ramassage *m* des ordures; enlèvement *m* des ordures; voirie *f*
refuse tip décharge *f*; dépotoir *m*
region domaine *m*
registered address domicile *m* principal
registration (law) transcription *f*
registration fees droits *mpl* d'enregistrement
regulate (to) régler *v*
regulation(s) réglementation *f*; règlement *m*
release of debt décharge *f*
relief dégrèvement *m*
remit (to) (funds) remettre *v*; verser *v*
remittance versement *m*
removal (furniture) déménagement *m*
render (to) crépir *v*; plâtrer *v*
rendering crépi *m*; ravalement *m*; crépissage *m*
renewal reconduction *f*
renewal (of a loan) prorogation *f*
renounce (to) renoncer *v*
renovate (to) rénover *v*
renovation rénovation *f*
rent/rental loyer *m*; rente *f*; redevance *f*
rent (to) louer *v*; prendre *v* en location
rent agreement contrat *m* de location
rent paid for use of arable land fermage *m*
rental (telephone, flat etc) abonnement *m*
rental charge redevance *f*
renter locataire *f*
renting location *f*
repair (to) réparer *v*
repairing réfection *f*; réparation *f*
replace (to) remplacer *v*; remettre *v*; replacer *v*
report compte-rendu *m*
report of state of accommodation état *m* des lieux
report or statement procès-verbal *m*; procès-verbaux *mpl*
report or statement (spoken or written)

constat [‡] *m*

representative interlocuteur *m*; interlocutrice *f*; syndic *m*

rescinding résiliation *f*

research (to) rechercher *v*

reservation contract (eg for purchase of a property being built) contrat *m* de reservation

reserve réserve *f*

reservoir réservoir *m*

residence résidence *f*; demeure *f*; logis *m*

resident's permit carte *f* de séjour

residential flats résidence *f*

resolutive clause clause *f* résolutoire

restart (to) (a machine) remettre *v*

restoration restauration *f*; rénovation *f*; ravalement *m*; réfection *f*

restoration of goods mainlevée *f*

restore (to) restaurer *v*; rénover *v*

resurfacing ravalement *m*

retailer fournisseur *m*

riddance débarras *m*

rider (eg to a contract) avenant *m*

right droit *m*

right of way droit *m* de passage

right to draw water droit *m* de puisage

rim rebord *m*

rise (to) monter *v*

riser (of stair) contremarche *f*; montant *m*

river/major river fleuve *m*

riverlet ruisseau *m*

road route [+] *f*; rue *f*; chaussée *f*

roadworks chantier *m*

roof toit *m*; toiture *f*; couverture *f*

roof (cover and frame) comble [+] *m*

roof covering couverture *f*

roof space comble [+] *m*; combles *mpl*

roof tiler couvreur *m*

roof timbers ferme *f*

roof truss ferme *f*; armature *f* à toit

roof trussing comble [+] *m*

roofer couvreur *m*

roofing toiture *f*; couverture *f*

room salle [+] *f*; pièce *f*

room, maid's chambre *f* de bonne

room, spare/guest chambre *f* d'amis

rough sketch ébauche *f*; esquisse *f*

roughcast crépi *m*

roughcasting ravalenent *m*; crépissage *m*

route route *f*

rub down (to) poncer *v*

rubbing down ponçage *m*

rubbish détritus *mpl*

rubbish (household) ordures *fpl*; ordures *flp* ménagères

rubbish dump/tip dépotoir *m*; décharge *f*; voirie *f*

rubble décombres *mpl*; gravats *mpl*; gravois *m*

rubble work; filling-in (of wall) blocage *m*

rubble-stone moellon *m*

rust rouille [+] *f*

rustic cottage maisonnette *f*

S

sagging affaissement *m*

sale vente [+] *f*

sale (shop) solde *m*

sale goods solde *m*

sand sable [+] *m*

sand down (to) poncer *v*

sandblast (to) sabler *v*

sandblasting; sanding sablage *m*

sander/sanding machine ponceuse *f*

sanding (down) ponçage *m*

sandpaper (to) poncer *v*

sandpapering ponçage *m*

sanitary sanitaire *adj*

sanitation assainissement *m*

scie scie *f*

sawmill scierie *f*

scaffolding échafaudage *m*

scale gamme *f*

scale (eg of map) échelle *f*

scale drawing plan *m*

scale of charges barème [‡] *m*

scenery paysage *m*

scheme schéma *m*; schème *m*; projet *m*

school école [+] *f*

scour (to) nettoyer *v*

screed chape ciment *f*

screen (to) (elect) blinder *v*

screening (elect) blindage *m*

screw vis *f*

screwdriver tournevis *m*

scrub (undergrowth) broussailles *fpl*

scrub on hillside (Mediterranean) garrigue *f*

scrubland garrigue *f*

scullery arrière-cuisine *f*; souillarde *f*

sea mer *f*
sea level niveau *m* de la mer
seal joint *m*
seal (to) sceller *v*
search for (to) rechercher *v*
seat siège *m*
section/cross-section coupe *f*
sector secteur *m*
secure (to) assujettir *v*
security nantissement *m*; caution *f*; garantie *f*
seek (to) rechercher *v*
seizure mainmise *f*
seizure (court order) saisie *f*
sell by auction (to) vendre *v* aux enchères
seller vendeur *m*
semi-detached house maison *f* jumelle
semi-detached houses maisons *fpl* mitoyennes
sequestration séquestre *m*
sequestrator séquestre *m*
series gamme *f*
service service *m*; prestation *f*
service (to) entretenir *v*
service charges (payable by tenants of flats etc) charges *fpl* d'un appartement
servicing entretien *m*
serving hatch passe-plat(s) *m*
setting out implantation *f*
setting up mise *f* en œuvre
settle (to) (a bill) verser *v*; régler *v*
settlement versement *m*; règlement *m*; apurement *m*
settlement date échéance *f*
sewage disposal assainissement *m*
sewage works dépotoir *m*
sewer égout *m*
shade (blind) store *m*
shade (colour) coloris *m*; teinte *f*
shaft puits *m*
shaft (mech) arbre *m*
share quotité *f*; quote-part *f*
share (to) partager *v*
sharing partage *m*
sharing out répartition *f*
shed abri *m*; appentis *m*; hangar *m*; chai *m*; remise *f*
sheet metal tôle *f*
sheet-metal workshop tôlerie *f*
sheet (eg of plasterboard) plaque *f*
sheeting (wood or metal, used to shore excavation) blindage *m*

shelf étagère *f*
shell (eg of a building) gros œuvre *m*; carcasse *f*; voile *f*
shelter abri *m*
shift (to) déplacer *v*
shop magasin *m*
shore up (to) blinder *v*
shoring up blindage *m*
shovel/spade pelle *f*
shower douche ⁺ *f*
shower tray bac *m* de douche
shower unit bloc-douche *m*
shut clos,-e *adj*
shutter volet ⁺ *m*; contrevent *m*; persienne *f*
side-timber panne *f*
sign (to) signer *v*
signature signature *f*
signing (a contract, deed) passation *f*
sill seuil *m*
sink évier *m*; bac *m*
sinking (eg of walls) affaissement *m*
site with services laid on terrain *m* viabilisé
siting implantation *f*
sitting room salon *m*
size taille *f*
sketch esquisse *f*; dessin *m*; schéma *m*; schème
skirting board/skirting plinthe *f*
skylight claire-voie *f*; tabatière *f*; lanterneau *m*
slab dalle *f*
slate (roofing) ardoise *f*; also *adj*
slate (to) couvrir *v* un toit d'ardoises; ardoiser *v*
slater couvreur *m*
sledge hammer masse *f*
slip bordereau *m*; talon *m*
slope pente *f*; chute *f*
sloping roof appentis *m*
small courtyard courette *f*
small farmhouse fermette *f*; mas *m*; mazet *m*
small flat in town pied-à-terre *m*
small hotel logis *m*
small house maisonnette *f*; panty *m*
small stone hut mazet *m*
small wood bosquet *m*
smooth (to) ragréer *v*
smooth (to)/smooth down (to) lisser *v*
smoothing lissage *m*
soak away puisard *m*
soaking douche *f*

socket prise *f*
socket outlet (elect) socle *m*
soil sol *m*; terre *f*
sojourn séjour *m*
solicitor (conveyancing) notaire *m*
sound bruit [‡] *m*
source origine *f*
source (of spring water) source *f*
spacing between joists solin *m*
spanner clé ou clef *f*
speaker interlocuteur *m*; interlocutrice *f*
specialist expert *m*
specification spécification *f*; devis [‡] *m*
specified item prescription *f*; stipulation *f*
specify (to) préciser *v*
spinney bosquet *m*
split-level apartment duplex *m*
spring (water) source *f*
stable écurie *f*
stage étape *f*
stainless inoxydable *m*; inox *(abb)*
staircase/stairway escalier [‡] *m*
stairs escalier [‡] *m*
stake piquet *m*; pieu *m*
stakeholder séquestre *m*
stand socle *m*
standing (situation and condition) standing *m*
standing charge (gas/water supply)
  abonnement *m*
start (to) (eg machine) démarrer *v*
start/begin building (to) amorcer *v*
state état *m*
statement (eg bill) relevé *m*; décompte *m*
statement (eg of fact) énoncé *m*
statement of accounts bilan *m*
statute of limitations prescription *f*
stay séjour *m*
steel acier [‡] *m*
step démarche *f*
stepladder escabeau *m*
steps escalier *m*
steps (leading to an entrance) perron *m*
stipulate (to) préciser *v*
stipulation stipulation *f*; condition *f*; clause [‡] *f*
stock (merchandise) réserve *f*
stockist fournisseur *m*
stone pierre [‡] *f*
stone cottage/house maison *f* de/en pierres
stone courtyard cour *f* empierrée
stone house mas *m*

stone pier jambage *m*
stone-mason maçon *m*
stoppage obstruction *f*
stopper bouchon *m*
storage space rangement(s) *m(pl)*
store magasin *m*
storeroom cellier *m*; cave *m*
storey étage *m*; niveau *m*
stove poêle *m*; cuisinière [‡] *f*
straw yard/loft pailler *m*
stream ruisseau *m*
street rue *f*
street gully caniveau *m*
street level rez-de-chaussée (rdc) *m*
striking off/out (eg from list) radiation *f*
structure ossature *f*; construction *f*
stub talon *m*
studio atelier *m*
studio apartment studio *m*; studette *f*
study cabinet *m*; bureau *m*
subject to (to) assujettir *v*
subscriber abonné *m*
subscription abonnement *m*; cotisation *f*
subsidence affaissement *m*
subsoil/substratum sous-sol *m*
substruction sous-œuvre *m*
subterranean (passage) souterrain *m*; also
  as *adj*
suburb (inner) faubourg *m*
succession succession *f*
sum montant *m*; somme *f*
summons mise *f* en demeure
sun-blind store *m*
supplier fournisseur *m*
supply alimentation *f*
supply of water approvisionnnement [‡] d'eau
support (to) porter *v*
surface surface [‡] *f*; superficie [‡] *f*
surface (roadway, etc) revêtement *m*
surface area surface [‡] *f*; superficie [‡] *f*
surface trunking (elect) moulure *f*
surplus stock solde *m*
survey expertise *f*
survey report rapport *m* d'expertise
surveying métrage *m*
surveyor géomètre *m*; métreur *m*; métreuse *f*
surveyor (land) arpenteur *m*
suspensive suspensif, suspensive *adj*
swamp marais *m*
swimming pool piscine *f*

switch (elect) interrupteur *m*
switch off (to) (elect) éteindre *v*; couper *v*
switch on (to) (electric light, radio etc)
  allumer *v*
switch on (to) (electrical appliance) démarrer *v*
syndic syndic *m*
system réseau *m*

T

tank citerne *f*; réservoir *m*
tank (fuel oil) cuve *f*
tap robinet ⁺ *m*
tap trade robinetterie *f*
tapestry tapisserie *f*
tapping branchement *m*
taps and fittings robinetterie *f*
tax impôt *m*; taxe *f*
tax liability impôt *m*
tax list rôle *m* d'impôt
tax rate impôt *m*
tax-collector percepteur *m*
tax-collector's office perception *f*
tax-free hors taxe *adj*; HT *abb*
taxation taxation *f*; impôts *mpl*
team équipe *f*
ten-year guarantee on new property décennale
f
tenant locataire *f*
tenant farming fermage *m*
tender offre *f*
tenure jouissance *f*
term of contract condition *f*
terminal (electrical) borne *f*
termination résiliation ⁺ *f*
terms conditions *fpl*; termes *mpl*; énoncé *m*
terrace terrasse *f*
terraced houses maisons *fpl* mitoyennes
terrain terrain ⁺ *m*
thatched cottage chaumière *f*; maison *f* à toit
  de chaume
the aforementioned (in legal documents) ledit
  ladite; lesdit(e)s *adj*
thicket taillis *m*
thickness épaisseur *f*
thread fil ⁺ *m*
threshold seuil *m*
tide marée *f*
tied-up assets immobilisation *f*

tile (wall or floor) carreau *m*
tile (roof) tuile *f*
tile (to) carreler *v*
tiled floor/tiling carrelage *m*
tiler carreleur *m*
tiles carrelage *m*
timber bois *m*
timber (to) (an excavation) blinder *v*
time-limit délai *m*
time-share/time-sharing multipropriété *f*;
  multi-jouissance *f*
tiny room reduit *m*
tip pointe *f*
title droit *m*
tontine tontine *f*
tool outil *m*
tools outillage *m*
town ville *f*; commune *f*; agglomération *f*
town centre centre ville *m*
town hall mairie *f*; hôtel *m* de ville
town planning urbanisme *m*
tracing paper papier *m* à calquer; papier-
  calque *m*
track chemin *m*
trade union syndicat *m*
tradesman fournisseur *m*
transcription transcription *f*
transfer (money) virement *m*
transfer (conveyance) of property transfert *m*;
  cession *f*; mutation *f*
transform (to) convertir *v*; transformer *v*
translate (to) traduire *v*
translation/translating traduction *f*
transom (window) imposte *f*
trap door trappe *f*
tree arbre ⁺ *m*
trench fouille *f*
trim (to) (hedge) tailler *v*
trimming ravalement *m*
trip switch (elect) disjoncteur *m*
trowel truelle *f*
trunking (elect) moulure *f*
trustee séquestre *m*; curateur *m*; curatrice *f*;
  syndic *m*
tub bac *m*
tube tube *m*; tuyau *m*
tubing tuyauterie *f*; tuyau *m*
turf gazon *m*
turning on (gas) allumage *m*
two-roomed flat or apartment deux-pièces *m*

UVW

under the table dessous de table
undercoat (paint) sous-couche *f*
underground souterrain *m*; also as *adj*
undergrowth broussailles *fpl*
underpinning sous-œuvre *m*
undersigned (the) soussigné *m*; soussignée *f*;
  also as *adj*
undertaking entreprise *f*
unilateral agreement to sell promesse *f* de
  vente
unit élément *m*; bloc *m*
unpaid bill ardoise *f*
upholstery tapisserie *f*
upright (stile) (of door, window) montant *m*
usage premises/dwelling will be put to
  destination *f* du local
use jouissance *f*
utility room buanderie *f*
vacant position jouissance *f* libre
value valeur *f*
value added tax; VAT taxe *f* à/sur la valeur
  ajoutée; T.V.A.; TVA *(abb)*
vat cuve *f*
vault voûte *f*; cave *m*
vegetable garden potager *m*; jardin *m*
veil (to) voiler *v*
vendee acheteur *m*; acheteuse *f*
vendor vendeur *m*
veneer (to) plaquer *v*
veneer/veneering placage *m*
ventilator ventilateur † *m*
vertical wastepipe (below WC) chute *f*
vicinity voisinage *m*
villa pavillon † *m*; villa *f*
village village *m*; commune *f*
vine-growing viticulture *f*
vineyard vignoble *m*; clos *m*
viticulture viticulture *f*
void (archit) vide *m*
wainscot (to) boiser *v*; lambrisser *v*
wainscoting boiserie *f*; lambris *m*
wall mur † *m*; paroi *f*; clôture *f*
wall, inner/inside paroi *f*
wall, low muret *m*
wall, outer/surrounding mur *m* de clôture
wall (to) murer *v*
wall anchor; wall tie ancre *f* de mur
wall covering (textile) textile *m* mural

wall up (to) murer *v*
wallpaper papier *m* peint; tapisserie *f*
wallpaper (to) tapisser *v*
wall-plate semelle *f*
walnut noyer *m*
walnut wood noyer *m*
warden gardien *m*; gardienne *f*
wardrobe armoire *f*
wardrobe (for hanging garments only)
  penderie *f*
warehouse dépôt *m*; magasin *m*; hangar *m*
warp (to) (wood) voiler *v*
washbasin lavabo *m*; vasque *f*; cuvette ‡ *f*
wash-house buanderie *f*
washer (eg for tap) rondelle *f*
washing machine lave-linge *m*
waste/scrap disposal depot déchetterie *f*
waste pipe écoulement *m*; trop-plein *m*
water eau † *f*
water distribution network réseau *m* de
  distribution
water-heater chauffe-eau *m*
waterproof imperméable *adj*
waterproof (to) imperméabiliser
waterproof floor and walls of a basement
  cuvelage *m*; cuvellement *m*
waterproofness étanchéité *f*
water supply approvisionnement *m* d'eau;
  alimentation *f* en eau
water tank citerne *f*
way passage † *m*; route *f*; voie *f*
WC, water-closet; loo WC *m*
well puits † *m*
whitewash badigeon *m*
whitewash (to) badigeonner *v*
width largeur *f*
will testament *m*
wind-brace contrevent *m*
window fenêtre † *f*
window box jardinière *f*
window pane (glass) vitre *f*
windows (pl) vitrage *m*
wine cellar chai *m*
wing (of a building) pavillon ‡ *m*
wire fil † *m*
wire (mesh) fencing/wiremesh grillage *m*
wire netting grillage *m*
wire up (to) (eg piece of equipment) monter *v*
wiring câblage *m*; l'électricité *f* (colloq)
wiring diagram schéma *m* de câblage

with services viabilisé,-e *adj*
wood bois *m*
wood preservative xylophène *m*
wood strip, tongued-and-grooved lambris *m*
woodland bois ⁺ *m*
woodwork boiserie *f*
woodworm dust vermoulure *f*
woodworm hole vermoulure *f*
word (to) rédiger *v*
wording rédaction *f*; énoncé *f*
work ouvrage *m*; travaux *mpl*; œuvre *f*
worker travailleur *m*; travailleuse *f*
workman ouvrier *m*; ouvrière *f*
workmanship facture ⁺ *f*; habileté *f*
workshop, joiner's menuiserie *f*
workshop/workroom atelier *m*
worth valeur *f*
wrench clé ou clef *f*
write (to) rédiger *v*
write (to) (a cheque) établir *v*
write-off abattement *m*

XYZ

yard cour ‡ *f*; jardin *m*
year of construction année *f* de construction
zinc zinc *m*
zinc, cover with (to) zinguer *v*

HADLEY PAGER INFO PUBLICATIONS
French-English, English-French

GLOSSARY OF MEDICAL, HEALTH AND PHARMACY TERMS

Paperback, 2003, First Edition, 203 pages, 210 x 148 mm
ISBN 1-872739-12-1   Price: £12.50
- Provides over 3000 medical, health and pharmacy terms, including common illnesses and diseases, anatomical, first-aid and hospital terms. Brief aide-memoire definitions
- Pharmacy terms include medicines, toiletries, cosmetics, health and pharmaceuticals

GLOSSARY OF FRENCH LEGAL TERMS

Paperback, 1999, 114 pages, 210 x 148 mm
ISBN 1-872739-07-5   Price: £12.00
- Provides over 4000 French legal words and phrases associated with legislation falling within the Civil Code and the Penal Code, (eg house purchase and wills), but company and commercial legislation is not covered.

HADLEY'S CONVERSATIONAL FRENCH PHRASE BOOK

Paperback, 1997, 256 pages, 148 x 105 mm
ISBN 1-872739-05-9   Price: £6.00
- Over 2000 French/English phrases and 2000 English/French phrases
- Eleven conversational topic vocabularies
- Aide-memoire key word dictionary

GLOSSARY OF GARDENING AND HORTICULTURAL TERMS

Paperback, 2004, Third Edition, 72 pages, 210 x 148 mm
ISBN 1-872739-14-8   Price: £8.50
- The glossary includes nearly 2000 gardening and horticultural terms
- The glossary matches up the familiar French and English names of pot and garden flowering plants and shrubs which are not readily available elsewhere

HADLEY'S FRENCH MOTORING PHRASE BOOK & DICTIONARY

Paperback, 2001, 176 pages, 148 x 105 mm
ISBN 1-872739-09-1   Price: £6.00
- Asking the Way, Road Signs, Car Hire, Parking, Breakdowns, Accidents, Types of Vehicle, Cycling and Motor Sports. Extensive Dictionary
- Over 3000 words and phrases included

CONCISE DICTIONARY OF HOUSE BUILDING (Arranged by Trades)

Paperback, 2001, Second Edition, 256 pages, 210 x 144 mm
ISBN 1-872739-11-3   Price £27.00
- Dictionary is divided into 14 Sections covering various stages and trades employed in house building
- Over 10,000 terms in each language

The above publications are available through good booksellers or can be obtained directly from Hadley Pager Info by sending a cheque to cover the price (postage is free within the UK, add 10% if outside the UK) to **Hadley Pager Info, PO Box 249, Leatherhead, KT23 3WX, England**. Latest Publication List available on request.
Email: hpinfo@aol.com